Alchemy of the Mind

Manage Your Mental Health Naturally

Vanita Dahia

Testimonials

Written in clear jargon-free language, this concise volume offers an excellent guide to scientifically based alternative or complimentary treatment of high prevalence common mental health illnesses, suitable for the lay person and the informed practitioner alike. It is written by a Compounding Pharmacist with an extensive track record in clinical practice, research, teaching and advocacy of alternative therapies in the mental health field.

Dr Kamal Sanghvi, Psychiatrist

To live a life in which we express our emotions in the most balanced and harmonious of way, requires a sophisticated GPS system of the mind/body connection. Alchemy of the Mind is such a comprehensive guide, easily and effortlessly directing us to live not only an emotionally enriched life but a life that optimises our greatest intelligence. Everyone would benefit from reading and learning from this wonderful book.

Dr.Sherrill Sellman,ND, author, radio host, international lecturer

www.drsherrillsellman.com

Sherrill Sellman, N.D.

"Alchemy of mind is a comprehensive master piece which cover complex area of mind and related psychopathology in a easy read format along with practical strategies to intervene"

Dr Sanjeev Sharma FRANZCP

Consultant Psychiatrist

Perth WA Australia

This is absolutely one of the best books on Brain Health that you can buy. I have read a lot of material related to brain health, but here is the one book that sets everything out as succinctly as possible in a comprehensive and easy to read manner. It is definitely something I would give to everyone I care about. Incredibly informative book. If you value your health, you have to read this book.

Strongly recommended!"

Mary Cavaggion- NutriPATH Director

First published by Busybird Publishing 2016

Copyright © 2016 Vanita Dahia

ISBN

Print : 978-1-925585-90-2

Ebook : 978-1-925585-19-3

Vanita Dahia author of this work. The information in this book is based on the author's experiences and opinions. The publisher specifically disclaims responsibility for any adverse consequences, which may result from use of the information contained herein. Permission to use information has been sought by the author. Any breaches will be rectified in further editions of the book.

All rights reserved. No part of this publication may be reproduced, stored in or introduced into a retrieval system, or transmitted in any form, or by any means (electronic, mechanical, photocopying, recording or otherwise) without the prior written permission of the author. Any person who does any unauthorised act in relation to this publication may be liable to criminal prosecution and civil claims for damages. Enquiries should be made through the publisher.

Cover image: Kev Howlett

Cover design: Busybird Publishing

Layout and typesetting: Busybird Publishing

Editor: Scott Vandervalk

Busybird Publishing
PO Box 855
Eltham Victoria
Australia 3095

www.busybird.com.au

CONTENTS

About the Author	1
Author's Note	3
Gratitude	5
Alchemy of the Mind	11
Happy and Sad Brain Chemicals	23
The Addictive Brain	41
Liquid Gold	49
The Second Brain	55
The Good Mood Food Brain	71
The Wired and Tired Brain	89
The Sexy Brain	99
The Thermostat Brain	117
The Fat and Frumpy Brain	127
The Toxic Brain	141
The Copper Head Brain	155
The Meditative Brain	171
Is the Brain a Meaning Organ?	189
Don't Guess! Assess and Address	197
Learn More	207
What Next?	209
The Final Word	213
References	214

About the Author

Vanita is reflection of you, the reader, with an inquiring mind seeking joy and happiness the holistic way.

Her years of exposure to ethnic and traditional practices, customs, and medicines, together with her nerdy chemistry and scientific mind have culminated in bringing forth a practical solution to managing the mind naturally. In a word, she could call herself a psycho-neuro-endocrine-gutologist, if there even is such a word! Actually, this book is about neuropsychopharmacology or how brain chemicals talk to each cell in your body.

Vanita is passionate about the metabolic potential of neuro-biochemistry in mental health, balancing the 'happy and sad' brain chemicals with validated assessments and custom tailored targeted nutritional medicine. Feel awesome, healthy, happy, vibrant and vital naturally!

On a formal note…

Vanita is an integrative medicine clinical consultant pharmacist, naturopath and nutritionist. She is passionate about treating the body from the inside out, and empowering the body to heal naturally. Integrative medicine encompasses the allopathic and naturopathic medicine paradigms and has a valuable role in treating any functional, structural, mental or emotional imbalance with its broad range of remedies, as well as working beautifully as an adjunct to many other alternative and orthodox therapies.

Vanita is a board-certified fellow in anti-ageing and regenerative medicine and provides clinical training, mentoring programs and educational initiatives internationally.

She provides educational and mentoring programmes on functional pathology and integrative medicine to health practitioners through her association with Nutripath laboratories, Antiageing and integrative medicine associations, and functional pathology academy.

She acts as a functional pathology clinical consultant and health services manager providing in-depth technical and clinical consultancy and expert technical training incorporating assessment, interpretation and prescriptive guidelines.

She has more than 30 years expertise in compounding pharmacy, herbal medicine, integrative medicine and R&D in innovative formulary.

She incorporates her technical consultancy with pharmaceutical compounding knowledge together with herbalism, homoeopathy, Ayurveda medicine and energy medicine like pranayama & meditation to achieve the best health outcome.

Vanita received her training in anti-aging medicine through association and membership with the American Academy of Anti-Aging Medicine (A4M and A5M) and Professional Compounding Centres of America and Australia (PCCA).

Naturopath, functional medicine consultations and interpretations of test results are available.

Contact her on **www.vanitadahia.com**.

Author's Note

The purpose of this book is twofold:
* Firstly, to assist all those suffering with ill-health, bad moods, depression, stress and anxiety
* Secondly, to my peers and interested health practitioners keen to help their patients with mental health issues
* Although this is a fairly comprehensive overview of integrative medicine and science-based nutritional healing, it is not intended to diagnose, treat or cure any disease. The play of chemicals should operate like a finely-tuned orchestra – in sync and harmony within each cell of the body. The overview of chemicals at work in the body and mind is not conclusive, and is subject to much more enquiry and discussion. It is advisable for you to seek medical advice from a qualified and experienced healthcare professional. Application of advice from this book should be used at the reader's discretion. The writer accepts neither liability nor responsibility to any person with respect to injury, loss or damage as a result of using the information provided in this book.

Alchemy of the Mind provides guidance only. The opinions and treatment options provided are the responsibility of the practitioner and the patient.

Disclaimer

The information contained in *Alchemy of the Mind* is provided for education purposes. It is intended to support consultation with a medical practitioner and is not to be taken as the giving of medical advice.

The recommendations, ideas and opinions in this book is based purely on research, and the subjective personal experience of the author and that of esteemed colleagues.

Gratitude

'Feeling gratitude and not expressing it is like wrapping a present and not giving it.'
William Arthur Ward

I am grateful to all of my clients, patients and friends who have pushed me to get the word out there about the simplicity of feeling amazing with the correction of body and brain chemistries.

'Your voice needs to be heard,' they said. 'I have struggled for years on all sorts of therapy, prescription medicines, and finally feel normal.'

'You make the chemistry so simple; it makes so much sense and it works'

'I like the fact that you are so "sciencey"; it must be the pharmacist in you. You're persistent and your enquiring mind gets to the bottom of those methylation defects.'

My inspiration came from the success stories of clients who felt that they could enjoy life, have their families connecting with them, have their relationships back again, successfully got off their antidepressants, and returned to work with ease.

I am thankful for my Indian background and for having been born in South Africa. Through these backgrounds, I was exposed to the cultural nuances of African voodoo medicine and ancient Indian rituals, some of which have been scientifically validated in Vedic medicine and conventional allopathic medical paradigms. I thank those who could not afford their medicines, for it was this low socioeconomic group in Africa that made me step outside of my conventional training and compound more affordable natural treatment options, blending the old with the new in what we today call integrative medicine.

I am grateful to my colleagues and peers who collectively over the years have shared their wisdom, and, who continue to educate me.

A special thanks to my peers and colleagues who provided valuable input, Nutripath and associated laboratories for having the functional pathology tests available and the Functional Pathology Academy for providing education support.

I am also grateful for the love and support of my children, Mishan and Karishma, and the warmth of my extended family and friends who make my life rich.

I thank all those who have contributed to me finding the space, motivation and commitment whilst writing this book, particularly the guidance in the process of writing through to publishing.

Most importantly, thank you, dear reader, for placing this book in your hand.

What Makes Me an Expert?

I was traditionally trained as a conventional community pharmacist, and eventually needed further challenges by embracing compounding pharmacy. I got tired of the routine and felt a dire need to bring in a holistic approach to medicine by integrating allopathic with naturopathic paradigms.

I have over 35 plus years' of experience in health industry as a pharmacist, naturopath, nutritionist and an integrative medicine expert.

As a pharmacist, I have pioneered in compounding pharmacy, the art of making medication from scratch. My very first compound in Australia was blending specific amino acids in a targeted dose tailored for my patient to alleviate the severe panic and anxiety she experienced. Within minutes of the treatment, she had calmed and thought I was a miracle worker. It was at this time that I chose to study further in the area of tailoring medication to suit the individual and to study integrative medicine with scientific validation.

As a naturopath, I appreciated the value of certain herbs, vitamins, minerals, homoeopathic supplements and amino acids that played a role in either relieving or treating symptoms, and enhancing the effect of pharmaceutical drugs, or countering the side effects of those drugs. After all, many pharmaceutical drugs today are derived from herbs. For example, vincristine used for cancer is derived from the periwinkle plant; our codeine painkillers are derived from the opium plant; heart medication, digoxin, is derived from the digitalis plant; and aspirin is derived from the willow plant, and so on.

As a nutritionist, the value of what we stick down our throats is paramount to our health. Nutrition plays a vital role in how we feel within ourselves, how we manage stress, how we sleep, and how we dream.

As a board-certified fellow in anti-aging and regenerative medicine, my mantra became 'your biography is in your biology'. Integrative medicine is a science of blending conventional with complementary medicines using validated assessment tools and evidence-based targeted treatment approaches. It incorporates optimising diet, lifestyle and exercise interventions with a holistic approach. It aims to embrace physical, psychological, social and spiritual wellbeing.

As an Ayurvedic medicine practitioner, I went back to my roots to understand the basics signs of our doshas or body types and associated diets, health conditions, and cultural principles. The art of pranayama, breathing techniques, and specific yoga asanas have proven to be profound healing practices.

As an energy medicine dabbler, I have always connected with my source energy. The power of healing can be invoked by tapping into your own divine energy under any guise, whether it be reiki, pranic healing, neurolinguistic programming (NLP), emotional freedom technique (EFT), meditation, yoga, qi gong, tai chi, or any other modality. Our brains can be said to have measurable brainwave frequencies that affect the state of mind and emotions. At different stages of our day we transcend our brainwave frequencies from a theta and alpha state to a beta state. Music has the power to transform your energy to an alpha state – a state of relaxation and induction of sleep.

Mastering this balance using energy can be a powerful healing technique.

As medical science continues to grow, this information may become obsolete. The use of antidepressants by Big Pharma has evolved from monoamine oxidase inhibitors to SNRIs within a few decades. Today, we investigate new and old therapies which are either marketed or packaged as innovative advances in mental health.

I have read many books, papers, and publications on mental health, neuroplasticity, and neuro-endocrine-immunological imbalances. I wish to thank and honour my peers and fellow professionals, and will continue to research in this area to assess, manage and assist sufferers of mental health.

I am confident that you will at least take away one or two messages and action steps that you will be able to use in order to feel happy, healthy and vital.

How to Use this Book

Alchemy of the Mind is a practical guide to help successfully manage mood and mental health disorders safely, effectively and naturally. The purpose of this book is to share what happens to your mind when other organ systems are out of balance. My 30 plus years of integrative medicine practice has culminated in a clear and comprehensive resource guide for you. We peel each layer off as we investigate the core or the underlying causes of your mood changes. Although this book is aimed to be as inclusive and comprehensive as possible, there is much more to the science of the mind. Please see **www.vanitadahia.com** for further education modules and step by step guides.

Value to You

I would like you to read this text from start to finish to get the crux of the material in each chapter. You may use the checklists to gauge your health status. The checklists are merely a starting point to establish the need for you to delve much deeper into your chemistries.

If a chapter resonates with you, consider taking action with the appropriate validated lab tests and evidence-based treatment approaches.

Further details of assessments are available with resources and interpretation guidelines.

It is advisable for you to consult your healthcare practitioner to manage your mind.

Checklists and Questionnaires

Each chapter allows you an opportunity to evaluate your own unique imbalances and the appropriate assessments that can elucidate the biochemical and metabolic blocks that contribute to your moods. If you have ticked more than 30% of each category within the checklist, then take action: take the appropriate lab test and consult with a professional as a stepping stone to optimal mental health. Lab testing is a powerful validated tool to assess your current health status, reveal your unique biochemical imbalance, and give you clues to natural treatments to correct the chemistries.

1

Alchemy of the Mind

Why 'Alchemy of the Mind'?

Alchemy is based on the belief that the elements of life, namely air, water, fire, earth and space are represented within each cell of every one of us and throughout the universe. Alchemy is a complex world-view in which everything around us contains a universal spirit capable of turning lead into gold.

Alchemy could best be expressed as turning a bunch of vegetables into a delicious gastronomical delight of a salad.

Alchemy is thought of as the power or process of transforming something common into something special, transforming sadness to happiness.

Alchemy can be thought of as a medley of remedies from many cultures, from the natural to the chemical, enabling us to heal. I will share with you my passion and pearls of wisdom that I have collated over the years about what works for the mind and why it works.

Today, stress and depression are the leading cause of disability worldwide.

The explosion of awareness in the media, and in research on the mind/brain chemistry, and new technologies associated with mood management is testament to the growing body of science. To achieve a happy and balanced mind, it's essential that we balance all the components that regulate our moods. When the mind is in balance, we project positive thoughts, happiness, and operate with a higher state of awareness. When we're caught up in the closed lower-level energies like fear, rejection, worry, or anxiety, we operate from a small sense of self-awareness or contracted awareness.

The development of scientific enquiry in the area of brain and neuroplasticity and neurochemistry has provided major advances in mood management. So we now see new areas or fields of study in neuroendocrinology, neuroimmunology, neurogastroenterology, and neuroplasticity.

Not Another Mind Book!

There are countless books, articles, and much media on managing the mind through psychotherapy, meditation or self-help tips. There are organisations and programs aimed to deliver tools for managing the mind. Pharmaceutical interventions have expanded and progressed to assist in the management of complex mental health disorders.

Optimal management of the mind to me involves finding the imbalance, investigating underlying causative factors, then managing the balance of all organ systems. This book aims to show you how to find the balance in your brain chemistry. This balance cannot be achieved without optimisation of diet, lifestyle and exercise, together with employing the tools of neuroplasticity. The works of Bruce Lipton and Norman Doige on neuroplasticity confirm that the brain can change itself.

Alchemy of the Mind is aimed at providing a logical step-by-step approach to balancing brain chemistries and bringing all elements of mind management together to achieve happiness. A functional medicine approach to balancing brain chemistries the natural way! After all, we make our own brain chemicals from the day we're born until the day we die – as the brain continuously changes itself.

The brain communicates with all organ systems. 'My stomach is in a knot' or 'I have a gut feeling about this' reveal an intimate relationship between your brain and your gut. After all, essential brain chemicals are made in the gut. This is why we call the gut the second brain. Changing your brain can change your life and every part of your physiology.

Changing the brain can alter your stress hormones, your libido, your appetite, and lots more.

Mental Health in the Old Days

Mental health disorders came in many guises from lunacy, to madness, to hysteria. The sufferers of mental health disorders were often placed in institutions and subjected to isolation and severe crude therapies including electroshock therapy, which is still used by some practitioners today. The mentally ill were chained to their beds in solitary confinement much like a prison. Techniques that were used on the mentally ill included insulin induced comas, malarial infections and lobotomies.

Much has changed since then.

While mental illness may not be a modern phenomenon, our level of understanding and the prevalence of mental illness in society is greater than ever before. Alongside the genetic influences that stand behind some of these illnesses, there are also physical and chemical influences that can spark mental health disorders.

What's Normal?

Should we work hard to be happy? Do we have it all backwards? We identify depression as a disorder finding its roots in our childhood. Psychotherapy is aimed at identifying the roots of behaviour during childhood.

We create a sense of normalcy in mental health. Normalcy is the average of what? In our education system, we measure how fast or how well a child reads based on the average. Any activity outside the bell curve is considered to be abnormal. It is a well-known fact that certain individuals who have conditions associated with autism spectrum disorders (ASD), albeit that they may be socially inadequate, may excel at certain activities such as music, athletics or intellectual expertise.

Sir Richard Branson, Jim Carey, and James Carville are all famous people who have excelled in their fields and were considered 'not normal'. It is believed that famous inventors and scientists like Albert Einstein, Thomas Edison, Leonardo da Vinci, Sir Isaac Newton and many more were likely to have had ADHD. They had above average performance in their field, seemingly superhuman ability to hyper-focus for long periods at a time, and had below average performance in normal educational settings.

What Does Good Mood Really Mean?

By standards of conventional medicine, good mood is the absence of disease. Could moods be instrumental in changing our emotional states of happiness? When there are no identifiable symptoms of illness, a patient is said to be well. When illness does occur, it is deemed as a single phenomenon that has arisen independent of the rest of the body. Drugs may then be prescribed to either suppress the symptoms or treat the isolated event without consideration of impact on other organ systems.

Using nutrients and amino acids means taking a different approach to health. It means considering the inner workings of your body, where the effect of each individual substance facilitates a series of reactions elsewhere. These reactions are called metabolic pathways. Disruptions in metabolic pathways impact the mind, which when left unmanaged, cause mental health disturbances.

As children we are constantly told by our parents how to behave to protect ourselves from 'something going wrong'. The fear of the negative action has been preprogramed for us to perceive stress is a negative thing. The assumption of stress as a bad thing is wrong.

Focusing all our thoughts on the stresses of finance, work, or domestic issues takes away from a focus of attention to ourselves in the here and now. The sense of needing more, whether it be time or material things to make less stressful, is part of the evolutionary psychology today. Buddhist psychology actually offers a radically different perspective on stress. Stress does not need to equate to suffering. Stress is universal, and emerges from the constant need to be fed, not getting what you want, or not wanting what you get. Chasing after things or pushing away and resisting things is when you may suffer. The stresses have an underlying fear component. Perpetual fear elicits a constant flight-fright-freeze response that changes biochemistry.

The big question is how we can shift the flight-fright-freeze stress response to a more evolutionary balanced response. The stress of fear acts as a portal for you to wake up. 'What's the habit when I get stressed? What do I do when I am fearful?' The natural response is to go harder, go faster and keep trying. This does not always work as it eventually leads to burnout. The moment you shift your perception away from stress, fear or negativity, your heavy egoist part falls away, then you become available for what wants to emerge. This is when you could pause and witness your thoughts and develop the space to evolve. We know how to evolve because we have the intellect – the developed frontal cortex from a higher level of wisdom and life.

In a large study of 1200 Buddhists who engaged in practices such as meditation, it was found that the Buddhists were psychologically mindful and tended to have good health. Another study in Thailand has noted 'suffering' defined in Buddha's four noble truths appears on the surface similar to psychological stress and has found that meditation can help in coping with a variety of stressors. Those convicted to prolonged incarceration or even those sentenced to death often seek religious support for comfort and meaning when faced with such extreme stress.[1]

Pain Plus Resistance Equals Suffering!

Pain is part of life whether it be physical or emotional. Acceptance and working through pain, is part of growth and healing. Not accepting the pain creates an unconscious resistance to it.

On the level of thought, the resistance is your form of judgement presenting as fear, negativity or reaction. The intensity of the pain depends on the degree of resistance to the present moment, and this in turn depends on how strongly you are identified with your mind.

The notion of suffering is not a negative thing, rather a pragmatic perspective that deals with the world as it attempts to rectify it. The pursuit of pleasure can only continue as an unquenchable thirst. We are constantly exposed to wanting more through our media and can never totally quench our thirst.

The Noble Truths

The first of the four noble truths in Buddhism identifies the presence of suffering, and the acceptance and recognition thereof. The second, seeks to determine the cause of suffering. Desire, craving, pleasure, accumulation of material goods and ignorance lie at the root of suffering. Ignorance of not seeing the world as it is and accepting the positive aspects of your life. It is part of an undeveloped mind to be unable to grasp the true nature of things. The third noble truth is ending the suffering by changing perception of your thoughts and stresses. This can be achieved by changing attitude, embracing a spiritual life, or transcending to a state of enlightenment through tools like meditation. The fourth noble truth charts a method of attaining the end of suffering through right thought, right speech, right action, right effort and concentrated mindfulness.

The core Buddhist principles are no different from any other religious or psychotherapy practice.

When we struggle we feel pain. Resistance to pain perpetuates the struggle. When a chicken is hatching from its shell, it undergoes an ache or discomfort and pain as it pushes against the internal shell. Release from the shell, it brings fresh new life to the little chick. The recognition of the problem or the pain evolves into freedom from pain. The pressure of your life is a trigger for you to grow. Often you would hear of a cancer sufferer changing their perception of life and will start to view things in a positive manner as a result of the pressure of their disease. When the winds of pain get strong, do we snap or do we maintain some agility to flow and accept the pain so that it may pass as change is inevitable?

Modern Marketing of Neuroscience

The brain is used as a ubiquitous tool in modern marketing. PET scans, EEG and MRI scans are used to track rhythms of the brain, which can be stimulated upon exposure to an item of food. Neuroscience is turning up more and more in marketing and advertising.

Headlines such as 'The Blues Make You Crave Chocolate' or 'You Love Your iPhone' or 'Sex Improves with the Cuddle Hormone' have been used as neuro-associated marketing (or shall we call it neuro bunk?).

What is being measured is the activation of the insula, a point of feeling, love and compassion in the brain. What the marketers fail to disclose is that the insula is not only involved in love, memory, and language but also anger and pain. Perhaps we should be aware of the neuro bunk!

It's not all bad stuff! There are 'serotonin' cafes springing up in Melbourne, Australia, based on the premise that foods rich in tryptophan, which makes serotonin will provide the ingredients for the "feel-good" hormone. The ethos is based on simple, flavoursome, and wholesome foods which enhance serotonin production ensuring that mind, body and earth function at their best.

Common Disorders

A detailed description of mental health disorders is expansive and continually changing. However, some of the most common disorders are stress, anxiety and depression.

Depression isn't an illness with a one cause or one treatment. For some, the problem may be primarily psychological or social, for others largely biochemical.

Most people experience a mixture of both. Common biochemical imbalances that may induce a depressive illness include:

* **Deficiencies of nutrients (vitamin B3, B6, B12, C, methylfolate, zinc, magnesium, copper, essential amino acids and fatty acids)**
* **Neurotransmitter imbalances (serotonin, dopamine, noradrenaline, GABA, glutamate and histamine)**
* **Blood sugar imbalances (often associated with excessive sugar, sugar substitutes and stimulants)**
* **Food allergies and sensitivities in susceptible individuals**

The presence of one or more of these factors may aggravate a person's ability to cope with stress and thus be an underlying contributor to what might otherwise be considered depression of a psychological origin. Depressed people may be considered malnourished in that they tend to eat processed carbohydrates instead of essential nutrients necessary to make brain chemicals.

Anxiety

Anxiety develops as a result of danger or threat, presenting as panic and fear. Various phobias, such as a fear of heights or fear of confined spaces, are associated with varying degrees of anxiety. The capability to handle anxiety comes from the biochemical make-up and psychological resources to manage the stress and anxiety.

Is Depression a Crazy Phenomenon?

With life becoming more pressured and fast-paced, the development of mood disorders and associated mental health decline are on the increase. It has been recognised that around 1 in 5 Australians aged 16–85 years suffer from some form of mental illness.

The rates for medically diagnosed anxiety and depression have tripled in the last 10–15 years. Mental health disorders are also recognised as a disability legally upheld under the Mental Health Act. If left untreated, the effects of chronic stress, anxiety or depression may become quite debilitating, often leading to progressive cognitive decline and physical/mental disability. Like many other disease processes, there are commonly multiple underlying factors involved in the development of mood disorders.

Some of these may include:

* **hormonal imbalances involving thyroid, adrenal & sex hormones**
* **disturbed neurotransmitter biochemistry, particularly affecting GABA, glutamate, dopamine, noradrenaline and serotonin pathways**
* **nutritional impairment – either by poor food choices, gut dysbiosis or malabsorption**
* **environmental factors including both heavy metal and environmental chemical poisoning**
* **genetic factors involving polymorphisms in key genes regulating neurotransmission pathways**

The cost of depression and mental health disorders result in a huge strain on public healthcare costs worldwide. Mood disorders exist in every culture, in both sexes, across ethnic groups –throughout the world. Albeit that the awareness of mental health is becoming more prevalent in today's media, those seeking help might only be a fraction of the total number of sufferers. The help that sufferers are seeking may not necessarily suit them. A multifactorial approach is absolutely essential in addressing mental health disorders. In practice, some respond positively to the prescription medication they are given. Often a patient may respond positively initially, then find that their happy pills are making them sad again. A practitioner might increase their dose or add to the prescription pile. If the SSRI (selective serotonin reuptake inhibitor) antidepressant is not working, the practitioner may increase the dose or add another class of mood enhancer prescription like a benzodiazepine, anxiolytic or antipsychotic.

What Does It Feel Like to Have Depression?

Having worked in the area of neurochemistry, I have seen countless cases of people who function normally on the outside but are totally different on the inside.

Depression is society's deep cut that we are content to put a bandaid on and pretend that it's out there and not in your home.

Anywhere in the world, one person takes their own life every 30 seconds. Society would look at it and say 'so what' or 'that's so sad'. They would invariably continue with their lives soon after.

A mental health volunteer in Africa once reported that Westerners isolate, counsel in a sombre setting, and drug their patients to a state of numbed normalcy as opposed to the African culture of drumming, dancing and integration into the community. Different treatments with the aim of the same outcomes.

How often do you see a social media post saying 'I'm going through a really tough time!'? Or 'I'm struggling.' Instead we pretend it's all okay and post smiley faces.

Is depression a chemical problem or a psychological problem? Does it need a chemical or psychological treatment? Unfortunately, our research is not advanced enough to explain the functioning of the brain fully.

What does it actually feel like to be sad? These are some of the feelings that have been expressed by sufferers of depression, stress or anxiety.

'My face is a mask. I feel like I'm being pushed into a grave. The situation is dire and I'm scared. Every chore is a huge thing. What you would consider to be normal like making a cup of tea is a herculean task for me. The problem is I look normal on the outside. People around me cannot understand what's going on in my head. Sometimes, I'm aggressive and called psychotic. It feels like there is a bomb in my brain ready to explode.'

* 'I was afraid that people would see me for who I really am. They would see beneath my smile that I was struggling, or beneath my light there was darkness.'
* 'Depression is a slower way of feeling dead. This 'deadness' is a serious disability which is part of the suicide statistic.
* 'Ever had a nightmare that woke you from your sleep? At least you can get up and fall asleep again. I feel like I have a nightmare going on in my head even whilst I'm awake. These nightmares in my wakeful state are like devils that are so terrifying that the angels have flown away.'
* 'I feel sad; life is not worth living; I feel fearful, and lonely. I occupy my time in an unconscious state of busy-ness, relationships are crap, and I feel trapped.'
* 'I feel like there's a funeral in my brain, with mourners coming and going.'
* 'I fear myself, my truth, my vulnerability. The real fear is the suffering inside of you. It's the shame, or the stigma inside of others, embarrassment or comments that you may not be quite there.'
* 'When I'm depressed, I look and feel like a homeless person: unkempt, untidy, lazy and disabled.'
* 'I feel like I'm living two different lives. That's a life that everyone sees, and there's one that only I see. Depression is not feeling sad when something in your life goes wrong like when you lose a loved one or you don't get the job you want. That sadness is a natural human emotion. Depression, in fact, is being sad even when everything in your life is going right. It's a feeling that you live with, day in and day out. It's not like a sore toe that heals within days. The scariest part of all is that you become numb to it.'
* 'Depression is like having a grey veil for which you see the world in a haze of a sad mood. If only someone could take away this veil so I could experience the real happiness inside.
* 'Depression is an exhausting thing, it takes up your time and energy. The internal silence makes it much worse.'

Managing the Mind

We need to stop commercialising mental illness and understand the sufferer. We need to fight the stigma and the prejudices that is associated with mental health.

We need to stop the ignorance, intolerance, stigma and silence. The only way we may beat the problem is to embrace the ignorance and overcome adversities in mental health.

Our treatments have many limitations. Albeit antidepressants are effective for some, they come with innumerable side effects, which may include depression, the very need for that medication. We should be grateful that pharmaceutical companies have advanced in mental health treatments and medications. Perhaps we should be grateful that the depressed sufferer was not deemed mad and institutionalised in a solitary confined cell or burnt at the stake. On the other hand, ancient community cultures incorporated and supported their members with tolerance and love. There was no loneliness and isolation.

Alchemy of the Mind aims at unravelling the metabolic blocks in your neural chemistry by investigating upstream or causative chemistry aberrations that affect the organ systems intimately related to the functioning of the mind.

It starts with optimising the happy and sad brain chemicals (otherwise known as neurotransmitters)!

2

Happy and Sad Brain Chemicals

Are We in a Sad Mood Epidemic?

Do any one or more of these statements describe you?
* **Feeling irritable, anxious, depressed and isolated**
* **Tried antidepressants but they're not working properly**
* **Antidepressants are causing side effects**
* **Depression/anxiety is affecting relationships or work performance**
* **Can't be bothered with fun activities. It's in the 'too hard' basket**
* **Libido, appetite and sleep patterns are disturbed**
* **Becoming a 'worry wort'**
* **Mindless chatter in the brain**
* **Fluctuating weight**

If the answer is *yes* to any one or combination of these, you may be suffering from just one or a combination of mood disorders including anxiety and/or depression.

Jimmy's Story

Jimmy, a 27-year-old male had not responded well with his antidepressant SSRI medication. He had taken various SSRI medications in excess of 10 years and stopped his prescription medication three months ago. He presented with addictive behaviours and thoughts. He craved processed carbs and sugars in the latter part of the day. Past history was associated with childhood traumas, and physical and mental abuse. He had undergone a significant amount of psychotherapy and psychiatric treatment. He has since up-skilled and practised various mind-body medicine techniques and was open to exploring an integrative approach.

Jimmy's antidepressants made him feel worse, hence he was reluctant to continue treatment. He reported that he felt a lot more agitated and sad on the antidepressants. He felt that his medication affected his sleep, libido flew out the window, appetite increased. He could not focus and his energy was depleted.

How Does the Brain Send Signals?

Neurotransmitters are brain chemicals contained within vesicles or 'storage pots' within the presynaptic cleft. The storage pots contain all neurotransmitters, which are released upon a signal and transported across the neuro-synaptic cleft from presynaptic membrane to docking stations called receptors at the post synaptic cleft. Nerve induction will allow these neurotransmitters to travel along nerve sheaths to the organ of action. Predominant neurotransmitters released are serotonin, dopamine, GABA (gamma amino benzoic acid), PABA (para amino benzoic acid), adrenaline, noradrenaline, and glutamate. Neural transmission is elicited on a microsecond basis. After all, if you happen to touch fire, you will react immediately. The brain receives the signal, releases the appropriate neurotransmitters that communicate with senses, and muscles react and respond.

Brain chemicals, when they're balanced make us feel happy, alert, confident and focused. We are in control of our moods, reaction to stresses, and generally get on with life. We don't sweat the small stuff. We get things done, are positive most of the time and live in the moment. We cope with the busy-ness of life. It is often said, 'Give a busy person a task to do and it will be done.' These are people who manage their time, are task-orientated and results driven. There are those who keep climbing, run the rat race and forget to listen to their bodies, start to burn the candle at both ends, and become adrenally fatigued in time.

Neurotransmission or firing of nerve signals happens at the synapse and along the axon via the myelin sheath. The sheath is very much like a roll of carpet filled with good oils, technically known as essential fatty acids and neuromodulators to enable swift transmission of the impulses from one synapse to the next. The 'good' oils, especially DHA (docosahexaenoic acid) are essential for brain health as it is oiling the myelin sheath. The oils are needed as a medium to speed up neural firing like an unlimited speed freeway as opposed to a highway.

Neuromodulators on the other hand are the medium by which the neurotransmitters travel and fire across the neurosynaptic cleft, much like a boat, neurotransmitters travel across water to get to their destination. A dry dock spells trouble. Without water or neuromodulators, the boat will not go anywhere! Neuromodulators are specific amino acids like choline, inositol, phosphatidyl serine, phosphatidyl choline, and lecithin.

What Are Neurotransmitters?

Happy and sad brain chemicals are called neurotransmitters, which keep the mood in balance. Neurotransmitters are chemicals that communicate information from the brain to the rest of the body. Hundreds of neurotransmitters are stored in the brain as chemical messengers ready to roll into action when brain cells are activated.

These chemicals are released and travel through the neurons like an electric grid supplying energy to a city. The brain uses neurotransmitters to tell the heart to beat, your lungs to breathe, or your hand to pull away from the fire. Neurotransmitters are responsible for every feeling, be it mood, pain, pleasure, happiness or sadness. They control our energy, appetite, and muscle tone – every physiological function in our body. Neurotransmitters are involved in sleep and sex drive.

All these activities happen on a microsecond basis. Neurotransmitters also affect mood, sleep, weight, concentration, and gut function. The brain talks to every organ system in the body. The central nervous system cannot be optimised without correcting diet, gastrointestinal system, endocrine system and the thyroid.

The nervous system works on the basis that neurotransmitters need to be in balance. A bit like yin and yang. When they're out of balance, we have all sorts of symptoms like sadness, moodiness and depression.

These emotions are governed by an imbalance of excitatory and inhibitory neurotransmitters. The excitatory neurotransmitters are glutamate and your adrenal neurotransmitters called noradrenaline and adrenaline. Without the excitatory neurotransmitters we don't get up and go to work, run the marathon or perform the duties of the day.

The inhibitory neurotransmitters, on the other hand, are serotonin and GABA. Without the inhibitory neurotransmitters we can't relax or sleep. An imbalance of either the excitatory or the inhibitory neurotransmitters may lead to over excitation or over inhibition.

Altering one of the neurotransmitters can potentially throw the entire orchestra out of tune.

The orchestra is made of some key players called dopamine, the feel good neurotransmitter along with cuddle hormone called oxytocin, a happy hormone called serotonin, and the pain hormone, endorphin. Neurotransmitters work to balance each other to maintain harmony.[2]

There exists in the brain a multitude of genetic, neuro-modulatory and environmental aberrations that have the capacity to produce abnormal nutrient levels in the brain. Mental problems result when a severe deficiency or overload of nutrients are present. Understanding the nutrient load and its association with mental problems is essential to optimal balance.

The Focus

Though the focus is neurochemistry, the balancing of your brain cannot be optimised without addressing all the cofactors that are responsible for manufacturing brain chemicals. Psychiatry has made huge advances in recent years. However, psychiatry still needs a new direction integrating all contributing factors with current modalities.

This book presents a holistic science-based natural treatment system that can help people with mental disorders. Pharmaceutical medication has saved many a life and helped many families through illness. Prescription medicine may be necessary and perhaps essential for those with complex mental health conditions like psychosis, schizophrenia and mania. They do, however, come with side effects and adverse reactions. Most mental health conditions can be managed effectively and efficiently with specific nutrients, which also have the potential to enhance the effect of pharmaceutical medication. We do not aim to attach labels to the mental health condition but examine the innate imbalance and correct it. The need for balance of neurotransmitters is the cornerstone to managing mental health, no matter what label we choose to give it.

Getting to the core imbalance is paramount to correcting the chemicals in our minds. Most of us were born with all our physiology in balance and intact. We get it all wrong when we become stressed, or through diet and lifestyle that is not congruent with harmony at a cellular level and balance at a biochemical level. The prolonged 'getting it wrong' eventually develops into mental health conditions.

Antidepressants

Amongst the highest prescription drugs dispensed worldwide in Western societies are antidepressants. It is estimated that more than 80% of Western populations have sub-optimal neurotransmitter levels. Depleted levels of neurotransmitters can be due to stress, poor diet, brain toxins, heavy metals, gene aberrations, stimulants, and recreational addictive drugs.

The earliest research on neurotransmitters began in the 1960s. It was suggested that increasing the levels of neurotransmitters especially serotonin was found to improve mood disorders, particularly depression and anxiety. An understanding of biochemical pathways requires identifying the precursor neurotransmitters, amino acids and specific nutrients.

Antidepressants have progressed from tricyclic antidepressants, monoamine oxidisers, and benzodiazepines to modern day SSRIs and newer generation antipsychotics.

Replenishment of depletion of neurotransmitters require amino acid precursors and its nutrients. SSRIs do not fill the tank; however, they improve neurotransmitter function by slowing its reuptake. The development of SSRIs is rather recent. SSRIs like prozac were first developed in 1987 and SNRI (selective serotonin and noradrenaline re-uptake inhibitors) was developed in 1989.

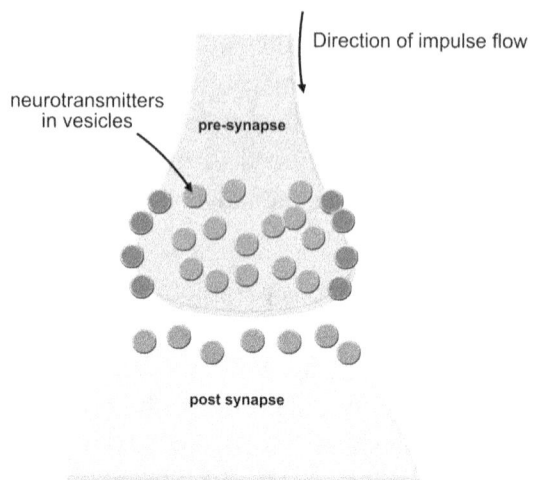

Most antidepressants work by altering neurotransmitter activity at the synapse. SSRIs bind to transporter proteins at the presynaptic cleft, which slows the exit of serotonin across the synapse. So the serotonin hangs around and is trapped in the synapse. This enables serotonin to be activated at the post synaptic membrane and hence increase serotonin activity.

A commonly used SSRI is prozac, also known as fluoxetine, but this has now progressed to include SSRIs like escitalopram, sertraline, paroxetine and fluvoxamine.

Benzodiazepines on the hand, interact with GABA receptors resulting in higher activity of the calming relaxing neurotransmitter. The commonly used 'benzos' are commercially known as valium and Xanax and generically known as alprazolam, clonazepam, lorazepam, and diazepam. They are classified upon the half-life or duration of action. Unfortunately, benzos use may develop tolerance and are addictive. Over time, you will need more of the benzos to have the same effect and may feel like a zombie the next day.

Biochemical nutrient therapy is a more natural method of balancing the neurotransmitters in the brain by normalising the concentration of nutrients, and amino acids needed for neurotransmitter synthesis, or to regulate epigenomic activity.

Neurotransmitters may be classified into two major classes based on its activity.

The excitatory nervous system is the dominant network in the brain that executes activity. Glutamate, dopamine, noradrenaline and adrenaline are excitatory neurotransmitters.

The inhibitory nervous system applies the brakes to the brain, slowing things down in order to relax, repair, and rejuvenate. GABA and serotonin are inhibitory neurotransmitters.

Inhibitory Nervous System

Serotonin

Serotonin is the inhibitory neurotransmitter known also as the happy brain hormone. It makes up 1–2% of the entire neurotransmitter production. Serotonin is necessary for a stable and happy mood. Serotonin is also necessary and involved in carbohydrate cravings, pain control, and sleep induction. Low serotonin is responsible for current epidemic of depression and anxiety. Most of the serotonin is manufactured in the gut, not the brain. Serotonin acts as a neurotransmitter as well as a neuromodulator by affecting glutamate excitation, stimulating its own receptors on GABA neurons, and inhibiting the release of adrenal hormones.

Serotonin is made from an amino acid, L-tryptophan, which is activated to 5-hydroxy tryptophan. 5-hydroxy tryptophan crosses the blood–brain barrier and has been shown to be effective in managing fibromyalgia, insomnia, headaches and binge eating.[3]

When serotonin is low, you may feel or experience:
* **depression**
* **loss of pleasure**
* **anger**
* **digestive disorders**
* **carbohydrate cravings**
* **insomnia**
* **low self-esteem**
* **migraines**
* **seasonal affective disorder**
* **constipation**

* worry
* anxiety
* obsessive thoughts
* irritability & panic
* phobias & suicidal thoughts
* fluctuations in energy

GABA

GABA is an inhibitory neurotransmitter that enhances relaxation and calm, acting as the brakes to the brain. GABA is known as a natural valium. GABA acts like a sponge soaking up excess adrenaline, draining away the tension and stiffness. Drugs and herbs that mimic the action of GABA are benzodiazepines, which increase GABA receptor sensitivity or valerian, which locks inactivation of GABA.

Alpha brain state is associated with meditation and relaxation. GABA significantly increases the alpha waves. GABA is synthesised in the brain from an amino acid, glutamate, an excitatory neurotransmitter. In the body, GABA is concentrated in the hypothalamus region of the brain and is known to play a role in the overall functioning of the pituitary gland, which regulates growth hormone synthesis, sleep cycles, and body temperature.

When GABA is low you may feel or experience:
* anxious and overwhelmed
* anxious and fearful
* disorganised or inattentive
* incessant worrying
* racing thoughts that keep you up at night
* heart palpitations
* cravings for carbohydrates, drugs or alcohol
* muscle tension
* panic attacks
* inability to relax
* burn out

The Excitatory System

Dopamine

Dopamine acts as both an excitatory and inhibitory neurotransmitter. Dopamine is synthesised in many areas of the brain, and is made from two amino acids, namely tyrosine and phenylalanine, together with iron and folate. If there is a methylation defect, the capacity of the body to produce your reward neurotransmitter is impaired even if the protein requirement is present. Dopamine is regarded as the reward hormone. Without dopamine, you won't salivate when you see the 'best bod' or see the 'best meal' in the world. No dopamine, no satisfaction! A lack of dopamine zaps the zest for life. Low levels of dopamine can make you feel tired, moody, unable to concentrate, and apathetic.[4]

A mild deficiency of dopamine can present as lack of satisfaction, or low motivation; a more severe deficiency may be associated with obsessive compulsive disorder (OCD) or in severe cases, Parkinsonism. Dopamine is a precursor for noradrenaline and adrenaline and also acts as a hormone when it is released from the hypothalamus, inhibiting prolactin production from the pituitary gland. In the central nervous system (CNS), dopamine is involved in the regulation of pleasure and reward, memory, motor control, sleep, mood, attention and learning. Low dopamine levels can result in impaired motor control such as, Parkinson's disease.

Low levels of dopamine are associated with all sorts of addictions, be it caffeine, alcohol, sugar, smoking or OCD type behaviours. Today, we have a new range of addictions that may be associated with depleted dopamine levels such as video games, internet, texting, shopping, gambling, power, work or money.

When dopamine is low, you may feel or experience:
* **depressed**
* **lack of energy, drive**
* **low libido**
* **lack of motivation or satisfaction**
* **mood swings**
* **obsessive-compulsive disorders**

- inability to lose weight
- cravings for caffeine or other stimulants
- lack of focus and concentration
- memory loss or inattention
- addictions of some sort

When dopamine is in excess you may experience:
- aggression
- schizophrenia
- hyperactivity
- Tourette's syndrome

Noradrenaline and adrenaline

Noradrenaline is made from dopamine. Copper and vitamin C play a vital role in the conversion of dopamine to noradrenaline. Copper is vital for synthesis of adrenal hormones or catecholamines. Too much copper, may have deleterious effects on methylation and mental health.

Noradrenaline requires methylation to convert to adrenaline. Noradrenaline and adrenaline are excitatory neurotransmitters as well as stress hormones. They are produced by noradrenergic and adrenergic neurons respectively, as well as by the adrenal medulla. They are most well-known for their involvement in the 'fight-flight-freeze' response, in that they increase heart rate, trigger the release of glucose from energy stores and increase blood flow to skeletal muscle.[5]

Low levels of noradrenaline contribute to a decrease in mood, energy, focus, motivation and memory. High levels are associated with aggression, anxiety, emotional lability, hyperactivity, mania, stress and suppression of the immune system.[6]

When noradrenaline and adrenaline are low you may experience:
- chronic stress
- adrenal fatigue
- depression
- decreased attention and focus
- decreased mood
- poor motivation and memory

When noradrenaline and adrenaline levels are high you may experience:
* aggression
* anxiety
* hyperactivity
* stress
* poor immunity
* manic episodes

Glutamate

Glutamate is a major mediator of excitatory signals in the brain and is involved in most aspects of normal brain function, including cognition, memory and learning. Glutamine is an amino acid that makes glutamate, an excitatory neurotransmitter. L-glutamine, the most abundant amino acid found in protein sources such as meat reaches the starving brain within minutes and can often put a stop to the most powerful sweet and starch cravings. The brain feeds on glutamine instead of glucose, which will restore energy and focus. Glutamine can act as a natural caffeine by rebuilding the neurotransmitter GABA.[7]

Glutamate regulates brain development and mediates lots of information for cellular survival. Glutamate exerts its function on a number of glutamate subtype receptors, which may then be associated with glutamate toxicity.[8]

When glutamate is in excess, you may experience:
* **excitable behaviour**
* **aggression**
* **anxiety**
* **cognition impairment**
* **signs and symptoms associated with deficiency of serotonin.**
* **seizures**

Play Between Neurotransmitters and Other Hormones

Not only do neurotransmitters interact and affect each other, they also work in balance with other organ systems. Your mood is not only associated with the brain, but also the gut, the adrenals, and your libido.

Tyrosine, for example supports deionisation of T4 to T3 thyroid hormones. Tyrosine also happens to be the precursor to dopamine. Depletion of tyrosine will invariably affect the thyroid.

Fluctuations in serotonin levels will affect thyroid-stimulating hormone (TSH) function on the thyroid. Serotonin depletion can also deplete TSH levels. Supporting serotonin with 5-HTP can increase TSH levels. [9]

Serotonin supplementation with an SSRI affects insulin, indirectly balancing noradrenaline and adrenaline or the adrenals. A balance of inhibitory neurotransmitters will influence excitatory neurotransmitters.

GABA and taurine relieve tension and support relaxation. DL-phenylalanine and glutamine can alleviate emotional pain.

Natural endorphins or pleasure enhancers may become deficient if you crave food or even need to numb the senses. Endorphins are natural pain killer neurotransmitters that can surge when you experience pleasure, say, with food, as an example. Foods that elevate your endorphin activity can often become addictive. So if you love certain foods you'll have a temporary surge of endorphins. Endorphins, known as the love chemical can be much stronger than heroin. Endorphins are released when you have the 'high' after running a race, the runner's high! They provide, pleasure, euphoria and joy.

Jimmy's Neurotransmitters

Jimmy has his adrenal status and neurotransmitter levels tested with a DIY saliva and urine sample kit.

His cortisol, the stress hormone, fluctuated outside of the normal reference range throughout the day, confirming the hyperactive state. Elevations in cortisol confirmed adrenal stress with fluctuations in energy, appetite, and agitation.

His neurotransmitters were flat-lined low across the board. Serotonin was low relative to GABA. Dopamine was exceptionally low. Noradrenaline: adrenaline ratio was highly indicative of methylation defects. Glutamate levels were low. Let's unravel Jimmy's results!

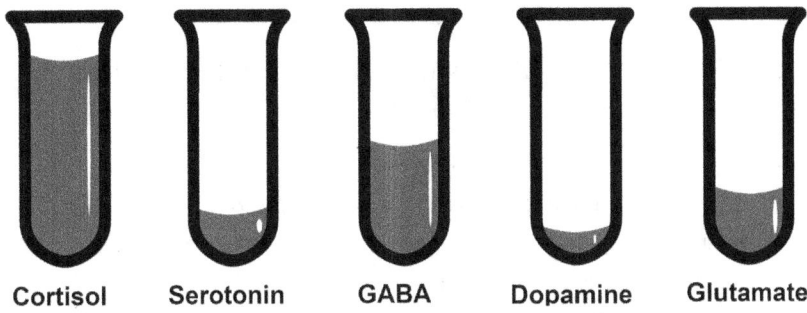

Prolonged chronic stress has put a strain on Jimmy's adrenals. He reported that his mind-body medicine techniques had got him to a point where he was ready to pursue the natural treatment approaches. Adrenal dysfunction in stress is typically seen in a pattern of high noradrenaline relative to adrenaline. The high noradrenaline to adrenaline ratio is seen in a flight-fright-freeze response or sympathetic nervous system stimulation. If the adrenal levels are not managed, a pattern of panic, palpitations or increased heart rate, shakiness and low blood sugar is often seen. He felt he could cope much better and feel less overwhelmed and less stressed with a herbal adrenal formula containing rhodiola, ginseng, and withania.

His serotonin levels was deficient despite recently stopping his prolonged supplementation with SSRIs. Over 70% of the population of serotonin deficient. Low serotonin is associated with insulin resistance and the need for 'sugar fix'. SSRIs will only assist in the serotonin pathway predominantly. In practice, upon pathology investigation, significant dopamine deficiency was seen as opposed to serotonin deficiency in depression. This explains why SSRI medication does not work for all depressed patients.

A depletion of serotonin calls upon GABA to try and balance the overstimulation of the sympathetic nervous system. This is often seen as low serotonin, elevated GABA and high noradrenaline.

Low dopamine is associated with anxiety and depression and is seen as a contributing factor to his addictions.

The first port of call is to balance the inhibitory neurotransmitters by supporting both serotonin and GABA with its precursors 5- hydroxy tryptophan, glutamine, vitamin B6 and SAMe.

Support adrenals with herbs, diet and lifestyle changes.

Support dopamine and GABA with L-theanine, tyrosine, phenylalanine, mucuna puriens, vitamin B6 and B1.

Jimmy reported improvement in his mental health in that:
- **he felt more in control, less stressed and agitated.**
- **he had a deeper sleep and felt more refreshed the next day.**
- **his low mood was alleviated.**
- **he no longer had the need for his 'sugar fix'**

Boosting Neurotransmitters Naturally

Boosting neurotransmitter production can easily be achieved with specific nutrients, vitamins, and amino acids.

Increase serotonin with:
- **amino acids like methionine, l-tryptophan, 5-HTP and inositol**
- **S-adenosyl methionine (SAMe)**
- **calcium, magnesium**
- **vitamins B2, B6 and D**

Decrease serotonin with:
- **folic acid**
- **vitamin B5**
- **vitamin B3**

Increase GABA with:
- **amino acids (like taurine, and L-theanine, found in green tea, glutamine)**
- **magnesium (considered as the body's nerve and muscle food)**
- **kava (a plant root effective for anxiety)**
- **zinc, vitamin B6 and vitamin B3**
- **GABA**

Decrease GABA with:
- **aspartic acid**

Increase dopamine with:
- **amino acids like tyrosine, phenylalanine, methionine**
- **SAMe**

* **vitamin B1, vitamin B6**
* **mucuna pruriens**
* **phosphatidylserine**
* **ginkgo, bacopa, curcumin**

Decrease dopamine with:
* **folic acid, vitamin B5, vitamin B3**
* **choline**
* **manganese**
* **GABA**

Increase adrenaline and noradrenaline with:
* **copper**
* **vitamin B6, vitamin C**
* **amino acids like tyrosine and phenylalanine**

Decrease adrenaline and noradrenaline with:
* **folic acid, vitamin B5, vitamin B3**
* **choline**
* **GABA**

Are Your Neurotransmitters in Balance? Take the Quiz!

Too much dopamine?
- *Developmental problems*
- *Schizophrenia*
- *Psychosis*
- *Possible increased testosterone production*

Too little dopamine?
- *Lack of motivation*
- *Focus*
- *Memory*
- *Addictions and cravings*
- *Low libido/decreased testosterone*
- *Poor motor control/tremors*

Too much noradrenaline?
- *Stress and anxiety*
- *Hyperactivity*
- *Increased blood pressure*
- *Pain*

Too little noradrenaline?
- *Lack of focus/energy/motivation*
- *Depression with apathy*
- *Adrenaline excess*
- *Insomnia*
- *Anxiety*
- *Stress*
- *Blood sugar imbalance*
- *Insulin resistance*
- *Allergic reactions*

Too little adrenaline?
- *Poor methylation*
- *Lack of focus*
- *Lack of energy*
- *Poor blood sugar control*
- *Glutamine excess*
- *Neurotoxicity*
- *Anxiety*
- *Stress*
- *Decreased mood*
- *Sleep disturbances*

Glutamine deficiency?
- *Fatigue*
- *Low brain function*
- *Poor memory*

Too much serotonin?
- *Headache, mental confusion*
- *Sweating, shivering*
- *Hypertension, tachycardia*
- *Nausea, vomiting*

Too little serotonin?
- *Depression/low mood*
- *Hot flushes*
- *Sleep difficulties/anxiety*
- *Carbohydrate cravings*
- *Constipation*

Too little GABA?
- *Anxiety*
- *Tingling of extremities*
- *Shortness of breath*
- *Numb feeling around the mouth*
- *Throbbing heart*

Calculate the number of answers you've circled against the total number of possible results. If you scored more than 30% of the checklist, you may have an imbalance. It is important to investigate your body chemistry with validated functional laboratory testing. (See Chapter 15)

3

The Addictive Brain

No addict wants to be addicted.

Addictions can take many faces, affecting people of any age race or sex and is most commonly associated with alcoholism, drugs and cigarettes. When you crave chocolate and cannot put it down until it's all finished, it is addiction! You may become irrational without your sugar fix. Prescription and over-the-counter pain medication, sedatives and stimulants are also increasingly being abused.

Tom's Story

Tom, 28-years-old, has taken to alcohol and marijuana in order to cope with his childhood trauma. Domestic violence, child abuse, a broken family home and lack of love were part of his upbringing. He felt he could cope with his job and life in general with the use of alcohol and marijuana. He is in a great relationship now and is keen to make it work.

He uses marijuana and alcohol regularly and is keen to get off them, following support and advice from his healthcare professionals. Withdrawal symptoms experienced when getting off his addictions in the past were feelings of depression, emptiness, frustration, anger, bitterness, bad temper, poor focus and bouts of moodiness. He is committed to taking action and getting off his addictions.

What Is Addiction?

Addiction is a chronic compulsive behaviour that can be harmful to the body. An addict adheres to their addiction to change everyday life from the unbearable to the bearable.

Addictions don't only include the physical things we consume such as drugs, coffee, chocolate or alcohol but may include behaviours such as gambling.

Psychoactive substances have the potential to cross the blood–brain barrier, altering the chemical balance in the brain. The psychological dependency can lead to feelings of guilt, shame, rejection, fear, anxiety and hopelessness.

Signs and symptoms of addiction can include:
* **insomnia**
* **increased or decreased appetite**
* **cravings**
* **social isolation**
* **taking risks**
* **obsessions**
* **denial**
* **hoarding**
* **financial strain**
* **relationship problems**

Is a Habit an Addiction?

An addiction is a psychological inability to control an activity. Habits are created through choice and repetition. A person with a habit can choose to stop and start. Habits are as simple as brushing your teeth each morning.

Addiction is habitual psychological or physiologic dependence on a substance or practice that is beyond voluntary control. According to the *Diagnostic and Statistical Manual of Mental Disorders* (DSM) in American Psychiatric Association, substance dependence is when an individual persists in the use of alcohol or other drugs despite problems related to use of the substance. Compulsive and repetitive use may result in intolerance to the effects of alcohol or drugs and development of withdrawal symptoms when use is reduced or stopped.

What Does Addiction Do to the Brain?

Addictions cause neurotransmitters to become deficient. Deficiencies or elevations of neurotransmitters have a significant effect on mental and emotional function. Repeated exposure to addiction disrupts neurotransmitter function.

Low levels of serotonin cause cravings, lack of motivation, anxiety and depression. Low levels of glutamate cause fatigue.

Dopamine depletion at the initial phases can cause addictions; further depletion can lead to repetitive behaviours as seen in OCD. Gross depletion is associated with Parkinson's disease.

Dopamine plays an important role in coding and predicting reward. Dopamine not only codes for reward but for saliency as well. Deficiencies in dopamine are associated with lack of reward and addictive behaviours.[10]

Glutamate may play a major role in cannabis addiction. Studies have shown that an amino acid, N-acetyl cysteine can regulate glutamate release, thereby reducing the cannabis seeking behaviours.[11]

What Does Cannabis Addiction Do to the Brain?

Prolonged use of cannabis or marijuana has been associated with altered connectivity and reduction in the volume of specific regions of the brain that are involved in memory, concentration, learning and impulse control. Most people who are addicted to cannabis function normally within the community. They may suffer from insomnia, anxiety, and mood disorders. Unfortunately, there are some who become psychotic after using cannabis. Recent research has found that marijuana users will carry a specific genetic variation, the AKT1 gene, which codes for an enzyme that affects dopamine signalling, and may be at risk for psychosis.[12]

Another reason for psychosis in cannabis users can be associated with a methylation defect, predominantly a gene variant for COMT (catechol-

O-Methyl transferase). COMT is an enzyme that requires methylation to metabolise dopamine and noradrenaline. The lack of methylation cofactors may lead to an imbalance of dopamine and noradrenaline, the very neurotransmitters that are affected by cannabis use – a drug use that has also been shown to worsen patients who have schizophrenia.[13]

Why Do People Have Addictions?

About a third of today's US population have 30% to 40% lower dopamine receptors.[14]

An individual who is low in dopamine will seek out substances and/or behaviours known to boost dopamine function. This can be temporarily achieved through alcohol, drugs, food, smoking, sex and gambling.

Alcoholics, for example, tend to be hypoglycaemic or have low blood sugar. They tend to forget what it's like to be hungry and interpret this feeling as a drug craving. Alcohol abuse often reduces appetite leading to nutritional deficiencies, predominantly vitamin B6.

Addictive drugs like opiates, which include codeine, ice, morphine and heroin, can cause blocks in the gastrointestinal system often causing constipation and impaired gastrointestinal integrity. Stimulants like cocaine and methamphetamine significantly decrease appetite, leading to weight loss and malnutrition.

Drugs like ice, marijuana and cocaine make you feel euphoric or 'high'. The brain stops producing dopamine once the euphoria wanes. Lack of dopamine leads to depression. It is at this stage that dopamine supplementation is necessary to counter the addiction of illicit drugs. Treatment after initial cessation is revolved around supporting the depressive mood and symptoms.

Ice, also known as crystal meth, is a stimulant that speeds up the messages going to and from your brain and belongs to the amphetamine family of drugs. People who use ice suffer from paranoia, hallucinations, memory loss and sleeping difficulties.

When the neurotransmitters are out of balance, the addict finds it difficult to satisfy cravings. They become progressively powerless. A sensible solution to addiction is addressing the underlying cause of imbalances of neurotransmitters. Chemical dependency changes the level of neurotransmitters that can result in the loss of memory, sleep, mood, agitation, depression, anger, fear. It affects the brain's ability to experience pleasure and pain.

One needs to avoid drug relapses by balancing neurotransmitters and the nutrients that support them.

All drugs of abuse target the brain's reward system by increasing dopamine. The overstimulation of the dopamine system will prompt reward in the form of satisfaction or euphoria, which then teaches addicts to repeat the behaviour. When some drugs of abuse are taken, they release up to ten times the amount of dopamine, initiating the behaviour of needing to take more again and again. After a while, the user does not get the same pleasure and has to increase the dose, so the body's tolerance to the addiction also increases. Over time the drug use depletes the brain of dopamine and the inability to produce dopamine naturally. The experience of pleasure becomes diminished. Eventually, the user no longer experiences pleasure from the substance and takes it simply to prevent withdrawal symptoms. When tolerance increases, the risk of addiction is much greater. The addict eventually feels flat, lifeless and depressed.

Unfortunately the prevalence of addiction has extended to food and media consumption and device usage.

A Sneak Peek at Tom's Addiction

The first step is the acknowledgement that he has a substance dependency problem or addiction. He has started psychotherapy, joined self-help groups and is progressing well. He has chosen to investigate his brain chemistry through neurotransmitter testing.

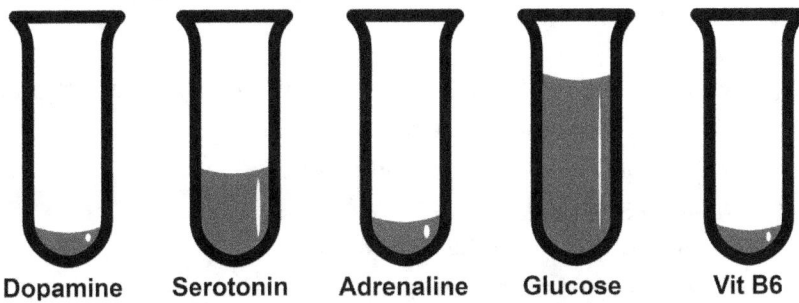

Neurotransmitter test results

Tom's urine neurotransmitter test results revealed that he had very low dopamine, low normal serotonin and low adrenaline levels. His glutamate was elevated. A depletion of dopamine is associated with addiction. Low dopamine correlates with low serotonin and poor mood. Dopamine is the precursor to adrenal hormones. Low dopamine will therefore lead to adrenal insufficiency and fatigue.

Tom's alcohol addiction

90% of alcoholics are hypoglycaemic. It's easier to start using alcohol when irregular eating habits cause blood sugar levels to rise and fall. This is why alcoholics should eat regular and frequent meals. Appetite wanes when addicted to drugs or alcohol. Alcohol reduces appetite and depletes essential vitamin B6. It causes an imbalance of fluids, electrolytes and impairs liver detoxification.

Addiction to alcohol or foods will initially raise dopamine, leaving a feeling of satisfaction. Continuing addiction to the stimulants will lead to subsequent dopamine depletion, which leads to a lack of motivation, reward and satiety.

Fixing Tom's addiction

Tom underwent psychotherapy and used neuro-linguistic programming (NLP) techniques together with exercise to manage the mind-body component. Although his diet was relatively healthy, he introduced more protein and vegetables in his diet. He managed his alcohol addiction with initiation of drinking three glasses of water for every glass of alcohol he consumed.

Natural treatment strategies for Tom

The primary principles of treatment based on Tom's test results are:
- **a down-regulation of glutamate**
- **an up-regulation of dopamine and serotonin**
- **supporting adrenals**
- **N-acetylcysteine for marijuana addiction**
- **fish oils for brain cell signalling**

Down-regulation of glutamate was supported with adenosine, which is a component of ATP (adenosine triphosphate) that regulates cellular metabolism and energy production. It was important that Tom reduced his glutamine and glutamate containing foods, which would be excitotoxic and neurotoxic to him.

Adenosine is an important neuromodulator that exerts its main effect on the brain through presynaptic control of neurotransmitter release. It primarily exerts an inhibitory effect on glutamate release, thereby inhibiting neuronal excitation.

Up-regulation of dopamine and serotonin can be supported with amino acids, predominantly 5-hydroxy tryptophan, phenylalanine and tyrosine and cofactors such as B group vitamins and iron.

Adrenals can be supported with herbs such as withania, Siberian or American ginseng, rhodiola, and rehmannia.

N-acetyl cysteine (NAC) is an amino acid that provides antioxidant protection and has been shown to be beneficial for paracetamol overdose and cannabis use.

NAC is used to treat various psychiatric disorders and addictions to tobacco, methamphetamine, cocaine, and marijuana or cannabis. NAC has been shown to restore normal regulation of glutamate release, which in turn reduces addictions to drug seeking behaviours.[15]

Addiction in this context is in relation to cannabis. However, many of us are addicted to activities or things we consume without realising it. Some may be addicted to work and struggle to balance their work-social-family life; others to caffeine or sugar. Without the morning coffee, you may not be able to function. Without the late afternoon sugar fix, you may not be able to complete your day at work.

Are You Addicted?

- *Have you used drugs other than those required for medicinal purposes?*
- *Can you get through the week without your addiction?*
- *Do you have blackouts or flashbacks as a result of your addiction?*
- *Do you feel bad or guilty about your addiction?*
- *Have you lost friends because of your addiction?*

- *Have you neglected your family or work as a result of your addiction?*
- *Do you have trouble maintaining work or completing your duties as a result of your addiction?*
- *Do your moods change when you've fulfilled your addiction?*
- *Do your moods change if you have not had your addiction?*
- *Have you experienced withdrawal symptoms like feeling sick when you have not had your addiction?*
- *Do you have medical problems as a result of your addiction?*
- *Have you sought any professional help for your addiction?*

Calculate the number of answers you've circled against the total number of possible results. If you scored more than 30% of the checklist, you may have an imbalance. It is important to investigate your body chemistry with validated functional laboratory testing. (See Chapter 15)

4

Liquid Gold

It's no mistake that when you have brain fog that you can be called 'fathead'!

Good oils, particularly fish oils, line most health food and pharmacy shelves. We become conditioned to think of fats as bad. Omega-3 fats, technically fatty acids, are essential to the human body and have benefits in the heart, brain, eyes and joints. Omega-3 oils act by reducing inflammation, assist in blood clotting mechanisms, and improve membrane function. It has been shown to assist in cardiovascular support, plaque build-up, in both persons with a history of heart disease and in healthy individuals. Omega-3 fats are important for optimal brain development in babies, mental function and particularly in later life. Omega-3 oils support normal visual development in the foetus during pregnancy. In short, the addition of omega-3 fats in the diet is important to maintaining both physical and mental health.

The brain uses glucose for energy, particularly in the absence of the good oils. The brain is actually fatty – it need the good oils, particularly DHA to function effectively.

Nerves that fire together will wire together! Firing of the nerves speeds up from one neuron to another along a fatty myelin sheath.

The myelin sheath is embedded in oil. Car pistons cannot function without oil, and similarly, the good oils/fatty acids are needed for your neurons. The good oil or fatty acids are the key fuel for the brain. It's not surprising that fatty acid imbalances can give rise to mental health disturbances. Our good oils are found in the body as omega-3, -6, and -9 in the ratio of 3:2:1. Omega-3 and -6 fatty acids cannot be made or stored in the body, so are therefore predominantly supplied by diet.

Our brain cell membranes are composed of over 80% good fats. They stabilise membranes required for proper brain cells to function. The good oils keep lining of brain cells flexible so that memory and other brain messages can pass easily between cells.

The link between low levels of omega-3 fatty acids and a variety of mental health conditions is emerging in the literature in the form of attention deficit disorders, depression, bipolar disease, schizophrenia, dementia, Alzheimer's disease, and mood disorders. Fatty acids are the key fuel source for the brain. It is therefore not surprising that fatty acid imbalances can give rise to neurological imbalances.

A brain cell membrane is composed primarily of lipids or good fats. Omega-3 and omega-6 fatty acids stabilise the membranes that are required for proper brain function. Our cell membranes are made up of over 80% of fat arguably the most essential of all the nutrients for the brain.

Lower levels of omega-3 oils in the diet can cause visual problems, learning difficulties, motor problems, and influence the ability of the neurons to use glucose. The good oils keep the lining of brain cells flexible so that memory and other messages can pass easily along the axon between nerve cells.

While it is essential to use omega-3 fatty acids, it must be balanced with omega-6 and omega-9 oils. Omega-6 oils are traditionally pro-inflammatory and therefore considered as the bad oils. If omega-6s dominate over omega-3s, it sets the scene for inflammation. Therefore, the ratio of omega-3, -6 and -9 should ideally be 3:2:1. Foods that support omega-6s include egg yolk, evening primrose oil, sunflower oil, olive oil, avocados, nuts and seeds.

Foods rich in omega-3 oils include flaxseed oil, fish, seeds, herbs like basil and oregano. Foods rich in omega-9 include olive oil, avocados, almonds, sesame oil, pistachio nuts, cashews and pecans.

How Does Omega-3 Affect Mood?

Omega-3 oils are related to a number of biological processes that are associated with brain functioning such as:

* **production of neuro protective factors that regulate the growth of new brain cells**
* **gene expression in the brain**
* **acting as anti-inflammatories, antioxidants and lubricating cell membranes**

Fish oils consist of eicosapentanoic acid (EPA) and docosahexaenoic acid (DHA), the latter of which is the main structural component of the brain.

Oil can go rancid. The typical ratio of EPA to DHA is usually 3:2. Small amounts of vitamin E can be added to fish oils to prevent oxidation of omega-3. Ensure that fish oil supplementation does not smell like fish as it may have oxidised and started to go rancid. Vegetarian sources of omega-3 include flaxseed, canola, soybean, hemp and walnuts, all of which are rich in alpha linoleic acid, the parent omega-3 molecule.

Recognising DHA's crucial role in neurological and visual development for infants has led to the inclusion of omega oil in infant formulations. DHA plays a vital role in the ongoing structure and function of the adult brain. DHA is a component of important phospholipids on the brain, the highest levels being found in phosphatidyl serine. DHA, in particular, is fundamental for brain development, particularly the sensory, perceptual, cognitive, motor neurone development. DHA enriches the membranes of the synapses and promotes fluidity of neuronal membranes, thereby influencing synthesis, degradation, release, and reuptake of various neurotransmitters.

What's Wonderful About DHA?

DHA is needed for proper function of nervous system. Our brain is 60% fat by weight and DHA makes up an average of 20% of all fat in our brain. DHA therefore accounts for about 10% of our brain's total weight. Depletion of DHA is associated with memory loss and impaired neurological development in children, Parkinson's disease, and severity of multiple sclerosis.

DHA is vital for:
- **healthy brain function**
- **brain development of a foetus**
- **nervous system development and memory**
- **management of psychiatric disorders, such as depression, anger, stress**
- **prevention of age-related memory decline and Alzheimer's disease**
- **brain signalling**

Which Fat Is the Right Fat?

The healthiest foods rich in omega oils are flaxseeds, walnuts, sardines, salmon, beef, soybeans, tofu and nuts. Omega-3s belong to a broader group of fats called polyunsaturated fats (PUFAs). The simplest form of omega-3 is called alpha linoleic acid (ALA). Like most vitamins, ALA comes from our diet. ALA in healthy individuals can be transformed into other omega-3s. In essence, our bodies need ALA, eicosapentaenoic acid (EPA), and DHA to stay healthy.

Natural Treatment Strategies for Tom

The most important oil to repair neuronal damage is DHA. Of course, any of the good oils in the diet should be optimised. Tom was advised to increase his dietary intake of coconut oil, olive oil, avocados, nuts and seeds. He included supplementation of DHA high potency liquid. He noted his focus and concentration had improved within weeks. His niggly pains had alleviated, confirming anti-inflammatory action of the oils.

Do You Have Fatty Acid Deficiency? Take the Quiz!

Do you have any of the following?
- *Craving for chips, cheese, rich food*
- *High cholesterol*
- *Liver or gallbladder problems*
- *Light-coloured stool*
- *Feeling heavy or clogged up after eating fatty foods*

- ◊ *Foul-smelling stool*
- ◊ *Dry skin*
- ◊ *Scaly or flaky skin*
- ◊ *Small bumps on the back of upper arms*
- ◊ *Lacklustre skin*
- ◊ *Stiff and painful joints*
- ◊ *Excessive earwax*

Calculate the number of answers you've circled against the total number of possible results. If you scored more than 30% of the checklist, you may have an imbalance. It is important to investigate your body chemistry with validated functional laboratory testing. (See Chapter 15)

5

The Second Brain

The Gut-Brain Connection

When the gut is in a good condition, food is digested, absorbed, excreted, metabolised, and detoxified optimally for the sole purpose of nourishing the body and providing energy.

The gut is considered to be the second brain, as the enteric nervous system lives in the colon. Neuro active compounds or brain chemicals are synthesised along with the immune system within the gastrointestinal mucosa.

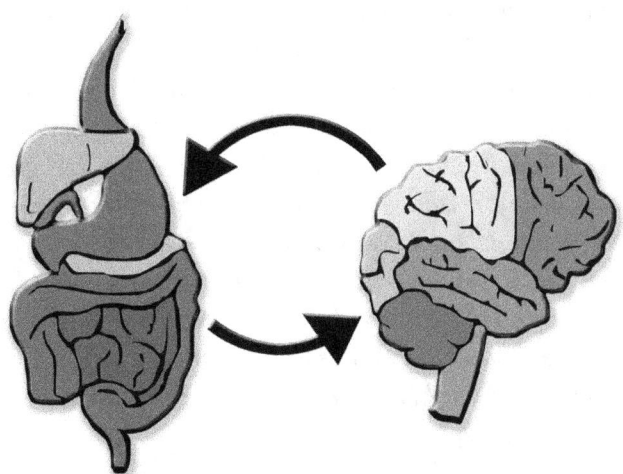

The Gut-Brain Connection

When stress affects the gut, it is common to say, 'My stomach is in a knot.' You may experience pain in the gut, constipation, or diarrhoea, or general discomfort. When the stress is alleviated, the symptoms may dissipate. The gut is considered the cornerstone to good health. It is in the gut that food is digested, metabolised, absorbed and excreted.

When the gut function is out of balance, many symptoms and conditions may develop which have the potential to develop chronic and serious health conditions unrelated to the gut. Symptoms may vary in intensity and duration depending on diet and stress levels. Typical symptoms may incorporate indigestion, malabsorption, metabolic and excretion disorders which can be rather uncomfortable and debilitating. The impact on general health and wellbeing can be detrimental if the gastrointestinal system is left unattended and managed.

Peter's Story

Peter, 45-years-old, a father to young teenagers, loves his work. He travels 70% of his working life to overseas destinations. He's an executive who is managing projects, people, and finances and is considered to be a high achiever. He has travelled for more than 15 years climbing up the corporate ladder. Three years ago, he believed that he had food poisoning whilst he was overseas. He was given a few courses of antibiotics to alleviate his gastro and flu-like symptoms. His tummy was never quite the same after his travels. He takes omeprazole for indigestion but has recently had to double the dose to relieve symptoms. He now complains of indigestion, belching, and bad breath, especially after he's had a few drinks. He used to be able to drink liberally but cannot seem to tolerate it these days. He goes through phases of constipation and diarrhoea tending more towards a loose stool. His flatulence is embarrassing at times and complains of feeling fatigued, possibly due to stress. He cannot seem to handle stress as much as he used to. He complains of 'going off the handle' more often. He feels overwhelmed with his tasks and seems to be on a 'short fuse'. He blames the stress for his periodic erectile dysfunction and lack of libido.

Responsibilities of the Gastrointestinal Tract

The gut houses the enteric nervous system – the second brain. In addition the gut is responsible for managing:

* diet
* digestion
* absorption
* metabolism
* excretion
* immune reserve
* microbiota
* liver function
* eradication of gastrointestinal infections

When the gut is out of balance, he may develop:

* **symptoms of indigestion, gastric reflux irritable bowel syndrome, bloating, constipation, or diarrhoea**
* **IBS – maldigestion, malabsorption, dysbiosis, and/or inflammation**
* **maldigestion – gas, bloating, flatulence, abdominal pain, constipation or diarrhoea.**
* **chronic maldigestion – bacterial/fungal overgrowth with alterations in gut permeability**
* **malabsorption – deficiencies of nutrients, proteins, carbohydrates and fats**
* **chronic dysbiosis – lowered levels of beneficial short chain fatty acids and altered bacterial metabolic activity**
* **altered GI immune function and exposure to bacterial pathogens – diarrhoea, mucosal inflammation, intestinal permeability, toxin production and auto-immune disorders**

Let's Have a Sneak Peek at the Second Brain, the Gut!

When food enters the mouth, be it fats, carbohydrates, protein or liquid, they're masticated with the help of saliva ready for digestion. Everything we eat needs to be digested by enzymes produced in the stomach, pancreas and gallbladder. These enzymes are predominantly amylase, lipase and protease, which digest starch, fats and proteins respectively. Additionally, the stomach needs to produce a sufficient amount of hydrochloric acid in order to break down food particles so that it can be broken down or digested effectively.

Peter said, 'I have indigestion and I'm belching when I eat certain foods.'

Digestive capacity decreases with age as we produce less digestive enzymes. Digestive enzyme production can also be reduced under stress or conditions of lack of hydrochloric acid production called hypochlorhydria. A depletion in digestive enzymes causes symptoms of indigestion, belching, gastric reflux and the feeling of food 'sitting in the stomach'.

Sufficient amounts of hydrochloric acid are required firstly, to provide the right acidity and secondly, break down food as it enters the stomach.

The conventional treatment approaches are aimed to relieve symptoms. They can be classified into proton pump inhibitors (PPIs) like omeprazole and pantoprazole, the older generation histamine antagonists like ranitidine or over-the-counter antacids like aluminium hydroxide, simethicone or Alka-Seltzer. Our forefathers were accustomed to use certain spices or teas like ginger, chai, pepper or even wine to aid digestion.

Unfortunately, the conventional treatments do not always address the underlying cause of indigestion. Instead, they relieve symptoms. Optimal digestion may be achieved with replenishing digestive enzymes or hydrochloric acid.

PPIs work by reducing the amount of acid made in the stomach. They are used to treat acid reflux and ulcers of the stomach and the duodenum.

The stomach normally produces hydrochloric acid to digest food and kill germs. Acid is corrosive and may break down the lining of the stomach or the natural mucus barrier protecting the lining. This mucus barrier breaks down allowing the acid to damage the stomach. PPIs work by blocking the hydrogen-potassium-adenosine-triphosphate enzyme system, also known as proton pump .PPI's are effective for symptom relief when used short term. If PPI's are used long term, the lack of stomach acid may lead to hypochlorhydria.

Hydrochloric acid is necessary to break down protein in the diet. Low levels of hydrochloric acid decrease the conversion of pepsinogen to pepsin, thereby decreasing the breakdown of proteins to amino acids. This limits access of pancreatic proteases to complete the digestive process. Lower levels of hydrochloric acid in the stomach can lead to anaemia and fatigue, reducing the capacity of the body to absorb vitamin B12 and minerals. It is therefore essential to get to the root cause of indigestion rather than bandaid the symptoms.

In the case study, Peter's indigestion was not relieved by omeprazole. Continued use of omeprazole had blocked hydrochloric acid production in his stomach. Supporting his digestive capacity with digestive enzymes and supporting hydrochloric acid production with betaine hydrochloride eventually reduced the need for omeprazole and relieved his indigestion.

Peter said, 'I go through phases of constipation and diarrhoea, bloating and pain in my gut.'

Irregular bowel habits are indicative of irritable bowel syndrome, pathogenic infestations, an imbalance of microbiota, or depletion of pre- and probiotics.

Further Travels Through the Gut

Digested or partly-digested food exits the stomach and travels down the ileum and duodenum into the colon. The colon is made up of the small intestine and large intestine. It's in the colon that peristalsis, absorption and elimination takes place. It's also in the colon that our brain chemicals are made.

The digestive material now passes the ileum and duodenum into the small intestine and travels along the small and large intestine which is large and lengthy. The small and large intestine when laid out can fill three football fields. It is therefore important to maintain gastric mucosal integrity. The action of the intestines is peristalsis, a wave like contraction and relaxation of the colon, allowing for absorption of nutrients and elimination of toxins. The wall of the intestine is lined with villi much like a corrugated iron roof. On the inside of the corrugations or villi there is a brush border, much like tiny hairs found on the inside of the nose. In the colon, bacteria, fungi, and parasites live in harmony within the gut. This is called homeostasis. Their job is to break down the digested faecal matter. The faecal matter is broken down into good nutrients that will be absorbed via the villi into the bloodstream and the bad putrefied and fermented material that is excreted through a bowel motion. An imbalance of beneficial bacteria or damaging pathogenic bacteria, fungi or parasites can develop dysbiosis in the gut. Dysbiosis is merely a state of imbalanced microbial ecology that leads to an overgrowth of microorganisms. Dysbiosis can inhibit nutritional absorption, impair immune integrity of the gut, and alter the elimination capacity. If you've had a prolonged course of antibiotics, these drugs will not only kill off the bad bugs or bacteria that have caused the infection, but also the good bacteria that are protective in the gut. This allows for an environment whereby other bugs like fungi and parasites may grow uninterrupted. This is the reason why some women who have antibiotics tend to get vaginal fungal infections. The fungi then have an opportunity to grow rampantly. In addition, the probiotics become depleted.

The 'Good Bugs'

The good bugs (probiotics) are necessary for restoration of essential microflora in the gut primarily to break down faecal matter in preparation for absorption or elimination Research has shown that probiotics are essential to manufacture important neuroactive compounds for proper brain function. The innovation of psychobiotics has been birthed from research and importance of probiotics in neurobiology. Probiotics are essential to the mind as they are needed to make brain chemicals.

Probiotics have now been shown to play a major role in assisting in alleviating allergies.

Likewise, specific strains of probiotics have been shown to be beneficial for certain health conditions.

When probiotics are deficient, you may experience:
- **irritable bowel syndrome**
- **gastric dysbiosis**
- **leaky gut syndrome**
- **flatulence**
- **bloating**

* **constipation**
* **diarrhoea**
* **pain in the colon.**

Specific strains of probiotics can:
* **help maintain healthy digestive function**
* **reduce the side effects of antibiotic therapy**
* **control urogenital infections**
* **protect against intestinal infections or pathogens**
* **help manage infectious diarrhoea or food poisoning**
* **improve immune resistance against other infections.**
* **reduce allergy and intolerance to foods**
* **assist in management of irritable bowel syndrome (IBS)**
* **support immune regulation in children with behavioural issues**

The Good Versus the Bad Bugs

The good bugs or microbiota are in homeostasis with the in-vironment living in harmony with the environment within the gut. The probiotics and immune system are adequate and in balance. In an unhealthy gut, probiotics may be depleted. Depletion of probiotics alters the balance of good bugs and microbiota that live in harmony in the colon to restore immune regulation through the microbiome. Probiotics serve to keep the gut healthy by providing good bacteria needed to break down faecal matter, protect the gut immune system and manufacture neuroactive compounds.

Bacteria in the gut far outnumber our cells in our body. The microbiome is a viscous thick layer of bugs within the lining of the colon called a pathogenic biofilm, much like a film in the mouth in the morning. We need microbes to survive. Unfortunately, we fear microbes and kill them with antiseptics and antibiotics. Food choices may be limited in variety which can diminish the bug population in the gut. We are loaded with bugs that can kill us. We need to learn to love our microbiome as they keep us healthy. Commensal organisms live in symbiosis, a state crucial to life. Bacteria, fungi and parasites live in harmony within the gut primarily to break down faecal matter in preparation for1 elimination or absorption by the body. The microbiome therefore provides primary immune defence to the body. If one group of bugs outnumber others, pathogenic infections develop leading to a disruption in the microbiome. Antibiotic use may be beneficial to kill off the pathogenic bacteria causing an infection, but may also have the potential to kill the good bacteria allowing for an environment for other bugs to grow in the absence of good bacteria. It is quite common for regular antibiotic users to develop fungal infections subsequent to antibiotic use. Probiotic supplementation would be useful to restore the balance of good and non-pathogenic bacteria.

Today we have the global threat of antimicrobial resistance. Bacterial infections that were once very easy to treat are becoming harder with antibiotic resistance. One of the main reasons for resistance is that food may be laced with antibiotics through agricultural process, an industry where antibiotics are often overused. Resistant bacteria pass their genes to other bacteria forming new antibiotic resistant strains, then bacteria change to protect themselves from the antibiotic, leading to what the World Health Organisation has called one of the biggest threats to human health today.

As superbugs develop, we would need to treat infections for a longer duration. Methicillin-resistant Staphylococcus aureus (MRSA) is commonly found in hospitals and accounts for many hospital post-op mortalities.

People with fewer bacterial species in the intestine are more likely to develop complications such as cardiovascular disease and diabetes. A flora with decreased bacterial richness appears to function entirely differently to the healthy variety with a greater diversity.

What Happens When the Bad Bacteria Outnumber the Good Ones?

Dysbiosis is a condition of imbalance of the microbiome, which may contribute to serious conditions like irritable bowel syndrome or SIBO (small intestinal bacterial overgrowth.). The science of probiotics has advanced to differentiate genus, species and colony forming units (CFUs) into specific therapeutic functions. Supplementation with the right probiotic can restore probiotic load and assist in its specific therapeutic function. Lactobacillis (genus) rhamnosus (species) has been shown to be beneficial in food allergy and skin allergy conditions such as eczema. One way probiotics improve the gut is by inhibiting the growth of disease causing bacteria.

Preliminary research reveals that several probiotics have the potential to alleviating symptoms associated with IBS. Let's explore some of the probiotics

A bacterial trilogy composed of bifidobacterium, lactobacillus, and streptococcus showed significantly less bloating and flatulence in two double blind placebo studies.[16]

Though the jury is out, specific probiotic strains may benefit certain gastrointestinal conditions.

Probiotics will do a world of good for the gastrointestinal galaxy. Probiotics in the diet have been used routinely in various cultures. Fermented foods and GAPS diets are gaining popularity as they contribute to a favourable microbiome. Such foods may include lentils, fermented vegetables, kefir, yoghurt, sauerkraut and kombucha.

Which Probiotic?

Not every probiotic is the same. They differ according to genus, species and strain. Neurochemicals have been isolated from specific species of probiotics, hence the term psychobiotics. Probiotics are instrumental in manufacturing neuroactive compounds in the gut.

Probiotic	Effect
Lactobacillus helveticus & Bifidobacterium longum	Reduces stress hormone, cortisol
Lactobacillus rhamnosus, Bifidobacterium	Increases GABA production, a calming and anti-anxiety hormone
Lactobaciillis	Increases acetylcholine production, memory, concentration
Bacillis, serratia	Supports dopamine production, the reward hormone
Streptococcus, E.coli, enterococcus, Bifidobacterium infantis	Increases serotonin production, much like prozac

Saccharomyces, bacillis	Manufactures noradrenaline
Lactobacillus acidophilus	Regulates endogenous opiods
Lactobacillus reuteri	Stimulates oxytocin production, the 'cuddle' hormone

Probiotic species have been shown to be beneficial for specific health conditions, as detailed in the following list.[17]

* *Lactobacillus rhamnosus* **is useful for skin conditions eczema, infections, allergies and immune support.**
* *Bifidobacterium lactis* **is useful for digestive immunity and allergies.**
* *Lactobacillus plantarum* **is useful for inflammatory conditions including IBS.**
* *Saccharomyces boulardii* **is useful for yeast infections, traveller's diarrhoea and antibiotic-associated diarrhoea.**
* *Lactobacillus acidophilus* **is useful for general re-inoculation especially after antibiotics.**

Probiotics do not work alone. They need to be fed by prebiotics to help restore immunity within the gut lining protecting the mucosa against inflammation.

Prebiotics are non-digestible food ingredients that may benefit the host by stimulating the growth of a limited number of bacteria in the colon. Prebiotics are found in a variety of fruits and vegetables like artichokes, asparagus, tomatoes, onions, garlic, leek, dandelion and legumes. Colostrum from mother's milk is the primary prebiotic immune enhancer given to babies upon initiation of breastfeeding. Examples of prebiotics and healing herbs used routinely in integrative medicine are lactoferrin, aribinogalactone, lactoalbumin, slippery elm, marshmallow, and colostrum.

They are necessary to improve the integrity and immunity of the gut mucosa. Prebiotic support is the cornerstone to treatment of all inflammatory conditions of the gut because the immune system lives in the gut. Synbiotics is a term coined from the use of a combination of pre- and probiotics. Conditions of IBS or IBD require support with synbiotics.

Peter said, 'My gut was never right after the food poisoning incident.'

He had a microbial or bug problem, so it's likely that his microbiome was compromised.

Examination of Peter's stool with a complete digestive stool analysis revealed poor digestion, deficiency of probiotics, small intestinal bacterial overgrowth and a parasitic infection.

His gut was 'not right' since he had suspected food poisoning. The most offending bugs contributing to food poisoning are parasites found in contaminated water and food.

Commonly found parasites in children come in the form of tape or hook worms. Parasitic infections in the gut can effectively be treated with anti-parasitic medication either in the form of anthelmintics or herbs. The brain becomes 'foggy' and serious inflammatory health conditions may develop when parasites enter the bloodstream and lodge in the organs.

Natural Treatment Strategies

Peter initiated the 4R program of therapy for his gut. It consisted of a systemised approach of getting rid of the infections and repairing the gut.

The steps in this detox program are:

* **Remove the toxins and offending foods, medications, gluten (if sensitive) and reduce poor quality fats, refined carbohydrates, sugars, and fermented foods, particularly if yeast is present. Antimicrobial therapy is given to kill the parasitic infection. Herbs such as oregano, phellodendron, clove, thyme, garlic and lavender were used with artemisia absinthium (a wormwood Western herbal medicine) for 1 month.**
* **Replace healthy digestive function and support gastric motility. Use herbs that aid digestion are deglycyrrhized liquorice, marshmallow root, and digestive enzymes such as amylase, lipase and protease.**
* **Repair the gut, treat the mucosal lining by giving support to healthy intestinal mucosal cells, goblet cells, and to the immune system. A**

complex of L-glutamine, liquorice, aloe, slippery elm and lactoferrins are given to heal the inflammation in the gut. Colostrum, sourced from first milking from pasture fed cattle, is particularly high in immunoglobulins A and G. Antimicrobial peptides, lactoferrin and lactoperoxidase and other bioactive molecules, include growth factors to support healthy immune function. Other prebiotics such as inulin, xylo-oligosaccharides, larch arabinogalactans, beta glucan, and soluble fibres may be beneficial.

* Re-inoculate with favourable microbes, the good bugs. Probiotics such as lactobacillus, bifidobacterium, and Saccharomyces boulardii are a good starting point to enhance the growth of the favourable bacteria. Introduction of foods rich in the good bugs include fermented milk products, yoghurt, kefir, and quark.

Peter's gut was maintained with synbiotic therapy, a combination of pre- and probiotics to put the right bugs back in, and improve the mucus integrity. He reported immediate relief of bloating and discomfort. Pain and discomfort was alleviated and he felt more energetic.

Peter was now ready to assess his liver function.

Liver Detoxification

I bet you've heard of detox or detox teas, diets and supplements. It's a term you've no doubt heard a lot of in the media, in magazines or at the gym. But why should you 'detox'? Detoxification is the body's natural process of changing dietary and environmental toxins into less harmful substances before eliminating them from your body. Supporting natural detoxification processes can help improve digestive function and may facilitate healthy weight loss; however, the benefits don't stop there – as healthy detoxification pathways may also lead to a reduction in other seemingly unrelated symptoms, such as sore joints or painful periods. Even if you're fit and well, for many people a regular detox allows you to feel more energised whilst reducing the toxin load.

All nutrients once they leave the colon are absorbed into the blood – we call this the portal system. The portal system is responsible for carting the nutrients in the blood to the liver to be detoxified. The process involves two major processes which are the phase 1 and 2 detox pathways that expel water soluble nutrients the body uses for energy and bodily functions to be excreted out via one of five excretory systems. Any metabolic block in the detoxification process can lead to accumulation of toxic matter, contributing to bad moods or inflammation.

Firstly, food matter passes through detoxification via cytochrome P450 enzyme systems that is known as caffeine clearance. This phase 1 process converts toxins that are absorbed via the colon into the portal system or bloodstream into intermediate soluble toxins.

These toxins undergo four conjugation pathways in phase 2 detoxification to produce water soluble toxins ready for the body to use as energy or be eliminated. This is why the liver is often called the 'engine' of the body that needs to be nurtured.

Powerful natural vitamins, minerals, herbs, foods and amino acids can assist in detoxification processes. The idea is to focus on supporting the main channels of elimination: liver, kidneys and digestion all to help optimise the liver's detoxifying capacity. Milk thistle along with cape jasmine and green tea help protect your body from the harmful effects of metabolising toxins. In addition, amino acids taurine and glutamine support liver detoxification pathways and promote a healthy digestive tract. Spirulina, coriander, kelp and aloe assist with the binding of toxins and promote alkalinisation, since an alkaline pH is required for effective removal of wastes via the kidney.

Herbs like dandelion, gentian, lemon balm and ginger not only help to minimise any existing symptoms of poor digestion such as burping, indigestion and bloating, but help stimulate the digestive secretions and bile flow you require for optimal digestive function.

Nutrients essential for optimal liver function are:
* **amino acids to support phase 2 conjugation pathways, namely, taurine, methionine, cysteine, glycine, glutamine, N-acetyl cysteine and acetyl-l-carnitine**
* **B-group vitamins, vitamin C, and magnesium**

One of the major conjugation pathways called glucoronidation requires calcium-D-glucarate to assist in hormone metabolism.

Prebiotic therapy helps support and encourage the establishment of healthy microbiota by significantly increasing the numbers of beneficial bacteria, therefore improving the overall microbiota composition.

From our case study, Peter was given a combination of herbs, nutrients and amino acids as part of a liver detox program for 1 month. He reported feeling clearer, lighter and more energised. He was recommended to repeat the 1 month liver detox program each year to 'spring clean' the body.

In summary, support the integrity of the intestinal barrier, provide healthy immune responses and promote intestinal microbiome homeostasis.

Is Your Gut Working Optimally? Take the Quiz!

Is your digestion good? Too little acid?
- *Indigestion*
- *Bad breath*
- *Belching/burping*
- *Poor appetite*

Too much acid?
- *Burning stomach*
- *Fell hungry after eating*
- *Heartburn*
- *Are you metabolising your food?*
- *Flatulence*
- *Nausea*
- *Constipation*
- *Diarrhoea*

Are you metabolising and absorbing your food?
- *Bloated*
- *Abdominal cramps*
- *Pain under right rib cage*
- *Diarrhoea*
- *Feel bowel not emptying*
- *Fibre helps or aggravates bowel movement*
- *Stress aggravates bowel movement*
- *Itchy skin*

Do you have parasitic infestation in the bowel?
- *Feeling unwell*
- *Pale skin*

- ◊ Rectal itching
- ◊ Achy joints
- ◊ Nervous
- ◊ Dark circles under eyes
- ◊ Vertical wrinkles around mouth
- ◊ Bowel urgency
- ◊ Indigestion
- ◊ Grinding teeth during sleep
- ◊ Itchy skin
- ◊ Travel lots

Do you have yeast overgrowth?

- ◊ Abdominal discomfort
- ◊ Depressed
- ◊ Vaginal itching
- ◊ Fatigues
- ◊ Fungal infections under nails
- ◊ Athlete's foot
- ◊ Foggy head
- ◊ Irritable when hungry
- ◊ Use antibiotic extensively
- ◊ Crave sweets

Calculate the number of answers you've circled against the total number of possible results. If you scored more than 30% of the checklist, you may have an imbalance. It is important to investigate your body chemistry with validated functional laboratory testing. (See Chapter 15)

6

The Good Mood Food Brain

'Let food be thy medicine and medicine be thy food.'
Hippocrates

Good mood starts with good food. We are blessed with a cafe called the Serotonin Eatery in Melbourne, Australia. The chefs have strategically crafted their gastronomical delights from foods that are rich in serotonin. After all, neurotransmitters are made from vitamins and minerals found in fruit, vegetables and amino acids found in our proteins. When the diet is wholesome, organic, and healthy for you, the brain can confidently top up the happy neurotransmitters.

John's Story

John, a 12-year-old boy, was diagnosed with attention deficit disorder (ADHD) and presented with typical symptoms, i.e. does not make eye contact, does not like being cuddled and repetitive behaviours. At first, he was a cuddly child playing with other children. The mother believes that he changed after his 2-year-old vaccination. He has always had bad breath, smelly stool and greater than normal flatulence. He bloats when he eats inappropriately and is highly stimulated and reactive when eating sugars or food with colours and preservatives. John loves his chocolate and is anaphylactic to peanuts. As he gets older, he strays from his strict wholesome diet, which is reflective in his behaviour. He becomes easily agitated, aggressive and irrational at times. He is currently on dexamphetamine.

His mum has done her research and proceeded to embrace functional medicine. She had his neurotransmitters and nutrient levels, metal toxicities and methylation gene markers assessed.

John's gastrointestinal symptoms like allergies and flatulence has a direct influence with his mental state. Gastrointestinal imbalances are associated with behavioural conditions like ADHD and ASD.[18]

It all starts in the gut! His diet, albeit healthy and organic, would need to be structured for him specifically.

John completed a diet diary detailing all he had consumed for 1 week. It was clear that when his mother managed his diet, he was eating mostly natural, wholesome food.

John would stray when he was with his friends or at parties. He was aware of his reaction, and would therefore limit intake accordingly.

John's peanut allergy implies that inflammation in the gut has contributed to flatulence, bloating and allergy. Bad breath, also known as halitosis, is a primary telltale sign of liver dysfunction or digestion. It is therefore necessary to restore gut integrity and improve immunity. Supplementation with prebiotics and probiotics would benefit John in improving his tolerance to foods, reduce inflammation and restore gut integrity. Investigating the need for digestive support and functioning of liver detox pathways is advisable with subsequent supplementation.

John loves chocolate, a delicacy rich in a neurotransmitter called phenylethylamine (PEA). These addictions or cravings contribute to PEA and dopamine depletion. Supplementation with PEA and dopamine precursors would benefit cravings and addiction.

John's family history revealed that his dad worked at the mines which may have contributed to a genetic predisposition to heavy metal toxicity. Heavy metals lodged in the brain are associated with mental health conditions and many chronic health issues. Strangely, John had supposedly reacted to vaccinations. There is much debate on the deleterious effects of vaccinations, particularly the use of thimerosal, a mercury containing preservative in some vaccines. It is therefore advisable to determine any heavy metal exposure through lab testing either in hair, blood or urine samples. Once established, appropriate heavy metal detoxification may be required.

John's gut and possible metal toxicities are contained in chapters within this book.

In this chapter, we will discuss John's food allergies and intolerances.

It is a well-known fact that food plays a major role in mental health. After all, neurotransmitters are made from specific amino acids and nutrients found in food.

What Has Food Got to do With the Mind?

Diet plays a major role in production of brain chemicals. The fundamental building blocks of neurotransmitters are contained in nutrients found in food. The relationship with food is the sum total of our innermost thoughts and feelings and what we eat. Emotions can govern the choice of food, like devouring a bar of chocolate or a soft drink. The brain uses more than 60% of nutrients from the diet to cope with stress and mental health. Stress and depression needs more food. A bout of stress can use much more fuel then a run around the block.

This relationship with food is deep and revealing. The many reality TV cooking shows are testament to tantalising taste buds and enticing gastronomical juices. The great Sufi poet Rumi once remarked: 'The satiated man and the hungry man do not see the same thing when they look upon a loaf of bread.' The food-mood relationship describes how the foods you eat can determine your mood.

Energy drinks or coffee for example, lift energy and stimulate alertness. Food like fruits and vegetables help to promote cheerfulness, satisfaction, and happiness. Other foods that have been found to boost mood include fish (including fish oils), nuts, and seeds.

On the other hand, processed and convenient fast foods, including canned foods, bread, sweets, chips, cereals, pasta, and alcohol can make you feel sad, flat, fatigued, angry or anxious. Feelings of sadness are sometimes accompanied by a craving for comfort foods, often rich in salt, sugar, or alcohol.

Specific foods are needed to synthesise brain chemicals such as serotonin and dopamine. Foods involved in manufacture of brain chemicals affect mood and is the cornerstone to managing the mind.

John's Allergy to Peanuts

The incidence of allergies (particularly peanut allergies) has risen exponentially in the last decade. Peanut products have been banned from schools and airlines for fear of causing severe reactions. A new study from the Murdoch Children's Research Institute proved that restoring the immune system in the gut with a specific probiotic known as lactobacillus rhamnosis allowed tolerance to peanuts in 80% of the children. 80% of the children who received the treatment of L. rhamnosus with controlled quantities of peanut protein were no longer severely allergic to the peanuts after 18 months when compared to 4% of the placebo group.[19]

Growing bodies of research are now providing promising support in the management of allergies and food intolerances with simple natural interventions.

Chocolate, Will You Be My Valentine?

Ever wondered why you feel quite blissful with a piece of chocolate in the mouth? Often just one piece of chocolate is never enough. You would want to devour the entire block of chocolate and are reluctant to share it around.

Chocolate has probably the most influential love compound called phenylethylamine (PEA). This chemical, which occurs in chocolate in small quantities, stimulates the nervous system and triggers the release of pleasurable opium-like compounds known as endorphins.

PEA, also known as the 'love drug', is found in chocolate and metabolised by the enzyme, monoamine oxidase. Prescription antidepressant monoamine oxidase inhibitors deplete the production of PEA. It's no wonder that chocolate has a calming and satisfying effect on the brain.

PEA exhibits mood enhancing properties, and as such, may be addictive. It may play a role in enhancing focus and concentration, improving mood and depression.

Addictions and Food and Mood

Are you a feaster, emotional eater or a craver? Did you crave certain foods when you were pregnant? Have you ever caught yourself eating foods that you don't normally eat? Have you eaten oranges around winter for immune support? The brain usually knows what the body needs. Compelling scientific evidence shows that mental and physical health are absolutely intertwined, and we now understand that the link between mood and nutrition is much stronger than previously thought. The prevention and management of many diseases rely on our genetic individuality, our environment, stress management, and healthy lifestyle habits – and nutrition is the foundation of a healthy body and mind.

Some basic food choice principles:
* **Eat a wholesome breakfast.**
* **Zone your diet to incorporate protein, fats and carbohydrates. Eat sufficient protein foods as they are building blocks to neurotransmitters.**
* **Avoid high-sugar foods or refined carbohydrates.**
* **Eat at least six servings of vegetables and two servings of fruit every day.**
* **Eat more of the good fats found coconut oil, fish oils, nuts, seeds, flax seeds and eggs.**

Stress busting foods:
* **Comfort foods like a bowl of oats can boost serotonin.**
* **Complex carbohydrates like whole-grain bread, breakfast cereals, and oats prompt the brain to make more serotonin and assist in stabilisation of blood sugar levels.**
* **Simple carbohydrates like sweets and soft drinks can spike up serotonin levels briefly. Don't make these a stress relieving habit.**
* **Vitamin C found oranges is necessary for neurotransmitter production. It strengthens the immune system and regulates the stress hormones.**

* **Magnesium found in vegetables like spinach is both nerve and muscle food. A lack of magnesium can trigger headaches and lead to fatigue, muscles aches and pains.**
* **Essential fatty acids like fish oils from cold water fish, olives, and coconut oil can prevent surges in stress hormones and help protect against cardiovascular disease, depression, and inflammation. The brain needs a regular supply of the good fats to stimulate neural firing.**
* **Choose beverages wisely: drink at least 2 litres of water daily to improve blood flow, enhance detoxification and keep the brain well-hydrated.**
* **Eat healthy snacks like vegetables, fruit, and nuts to keep blood sugar stable and provide energy.**

Which Diet Is Right for You?

It's best to choose foods that stimulate gut hormones to provide a feeling of fullness for a longer period. These are foods that are high in protein, such as fish and chicken, and low in glycaemic index (GI) such as pasta, lentils and basmati rice.

Have you ever tried growing your tomatoes as big and uniform as is found in supermarkets? The tomatoes that are homegrown may be smaller, may even be pitted and not uniform, and would generally tend to be nutrient dense and healthier than the commercial counterpart. Food today is either adulterated, or genetically modified.

Genetically modified soy or corn is used in daily diets across the world in foods such as bread, chocolates, potato chips, fried foods, oils, margarines, mayonnaise, and many others. Agricultural industries are using gene technology to improve the efficiency of animal production. This research uses the natural genetic variation in livestock to selectively breed animals that produce more meat, milk or fibre.

Awareness of modification, adulteration and agricultural processes of food should proactively give us the opportunity to make informed healthy organic choices.

Shall We Blame Our Genes?

Early investigations of gene regulations have revealed that nutrients can actually modulate gene expression. Ever wondered why a migrant who is used to their traditional foods then changes their diet, develop all sorts of food intolerances or allergies? A relatively new science called nutrigenomics shows how different foods may interact with specific genes, how foods 'talk' to our genes, and how genes express themselves after a conversation. The science of nutrigenomics confirms that food provides potent dietary signals that directly influence the metabolic programming of our genes and they also modify the risk of common chronic diseases. It's telling us which food contains instructions that communicate directly to our genes. External factors such as diet or stimulants such as smoking can interact with genes to increase the likelihood of developing allergies and subsequent diseases.

Generally, when the diet is out of balance, you are likely to experience:
* **fatigue**
* **cravings**
* **depression**
* **mood swings**
* **muscle aches**
* **nasal congestion**
* **water retention**
* **candida infections**
* **headaches**
* **insomnia**
* **indigestion**
* **leaky gut**
* **bloating**
* **skin rashes**
* **dark circles under the eyes**

Diets can be structured based on a fad, weight management, or health conditions. Novel innovations incorporating genetic profiling are now available to establish a tailored diet for you.

Some of the major classes of diets can include but are not limited to:
* **fad diets such as the lemon detox, 'skinny bitch' or grapefruit, 5:2 diet**
* **various promotional and commercial programs like Jenny Craig and Lite n' Easy**

* **intolerance-based diets for example, lactose free diet, fructose free diets, amine free or salicylate free diet, FODMAP diet, GAPS diet**
* **disease specific diets like inflammation diet, diabetes diet, stress busting diet, candida diet**

Do You Have Trouble Maintaining Specific Diets?

It's rather challenging to maintain a diet long term especially if it involves elimination of major food groups that are part of your regular diet.

Keep it simple! As a golden rule, aim for 90% of your food to be predominantly fruits, vegetables, water, good oils and protein. Protein can be in the form of chicken, fish, or meat or in the case of vegetarians, tempeh lentils, and mung beans. Good oils come in the form of fish, coconut oil, olive oil, nuts and seeds. Drink at least 2 litres of water daily. Take into account your specific food allergies and intolerances.

A Look At Some of the Pertinent Diets on the Market Place

Genotype diet

The genotype diet lets you zero in on the health and nutrition information that corresponds to your biological profile. You can make choices about your diet based on the dynamic natural forces within your own body. Dr P D'Adamo, founder of the blood type and genotype diet, has extended the blood type diet by tailoring diet based on the body's genotype and reprogramming gene responses. The genotype diet takes into account blood type, secretor status, blood group, epigenetic markers, and Lewis blood factor to establish a specific diet based on your genotype. Genotyping the diet has the capacity to lose and maintain weight, repair cells, avoid illness and age well.

The idea is to turn on positive genes and silence negative ones through methylation, histone acetylation and other biological processes. Using a diet tailored for you, you can change your genetic destiny by turning on the good genes and shutting down the bad ones.

Zone diet

This diet resembles a glycaemic index diet with the aim of weight loss. The theory behind a zone diet is a consumption ratio of carbohydrates:protein:fat of 40:30:30.

Paleo diet

This diet resembles the Atkins diet and is based on a simple premise: if the cavemen didn't eat it, you shouldn't either! The paleo diet contains no refined sugars, dairy, legumes or grains.

FODMAP diet

This diet is marketed specifically for the relief of irritable bowel syndrome or inflammatory bowel disease. Developed by researchers at Monash University in Australia in 2005, it's proven to reduce symptoms of fatigue, lethargy and poor concentration. Its acronym stands for fermentable, oligosaccharides, disaccharides, monosaccharides and polyols. FODMAP diet is made up of the following components:

* **fermentable** – broken down by bacteria in the large bowel
* **oligosaccharides** – 'oligo' means 'few' and 'saccharide' means sugar
* **disaccharides** – 'di' means two sugar molecules
* **monosaccharides** – 'mono' means single-sugar molecule
* **polyols** – these are sugar alcohols capable of controlling lipid storage

Alkaline diet

The pH of the body should ideally be around seven. When the body is stressed, anxious or inflamed, the pH lowers and becomes acidic. Prolonged acidity is corrosive to the body leading to pain and inflammation. Consumption of alkaline foods and reduction of acidic foods can regulate pH.

5:2 diet

This popular and fashionable diet is based on the premise of fasting for 2 days with calorie intake limited for 2 days per week and eating normally or regulating calories for 5 days. This theory is to give the body a break during fasting for 2 days per week.

Glycaemic index (GI) diet

The focus is to eat the good carbohydrates like cereals, fruit and vegetables in order to control appetite and delay hunger. Limit the bad carbs like white bread, which spike blood sugar making you hungry sooner. Glycaemic index is a measure of carbohydrate effect on blood sugar. Low GI foods digest slowly giving you a feeling of fullness for longer so that blood sugar and metabolism don't go out of whack.

Of course, there are hundreds of diets each with its benefits and deficiencies. There is no shortage of awareness of diets yet we get lured into comfort foods or knowingly eat foods that can easily be replaced by good alternatives. Be conscious of choosing the right diet, keep it simple by watching each mouthful.

Ketone Testing

Ketones are made when the body breaks down proteins. If blood sugar is high, it's usually an indication that you don't have enough insulin in your system to process the glucose. The body then starts to break down protein or muscle tissue for energy. Over time ketones build up leading to ketoacidosis which in turn, causes fatigue, muscle aches and pains.

Why Do Natural Mood Enhancing Chemicals Become Deficient?

Your body's ability to produce its own natural brain drugs are inhibited because you may have a genetic defect. Genes program the brain to produce certain amounts of mood enhancing chemicals. Your inherited genetic predisposition can present as traits in the family line. For example, MTHFR is a genetic measure of methylation defect.

Addictions will depress or enhance brain chemicals, which can further enhance the need for more food, alcohol or drugs as substitutes for the brain chemicals. Children of parents who have been drug users will often be drug users themselves.

Chronic long-term stress uses up the natural brain chemicals. Stress has a natural ability to regulate and protect the body. It does this by releasing cortisone, the stress hormone, and, in so doing, preferentially uses all the nutrients required for the adrenals to function correctly.

Excessive use of refined sugars, stimulants like alcohol or drugs and medication that alters the brain can inhibit the production of natural brain chemicals. These drugs may occupy the very receptor sites that the neurotransmitters are meant to be plugged into. In so doing, they reduce the amount of neurotransmitters produced, allowing for further neurotransmission or brain chemical drops, leaving a vacuum. This vacuum initiates a vicious cycle of need, and later, an addiction to various drugs.

Diet

You may be trapped inside a body that is malfunctioning. The body needs help. Years of dieting, psychotherapy and the best pep talks may not help. You might need a biochemical balance.

Steps to consider when adjusting diet:
* **correct brain chemistry**
* **balance blood sugar**
* **end low calorie dieting**
* **overcome addictions**
* **balance adrenals, hormones, and thyroid**

Food Allergies and Intolerances

Often people suffer with food intolerances and allergies and don't even realise it. End your many years of illness or inflammation! Delayed food reactions may be the underlying cause of your condition!

Airlines have stopped providing nuts as a snack; schools have removed certain food groups in their canteens; and each household is becoming more aware of food intolerances. The incidence of food intolerances, sensitivities and allergies has reached significant levels. What should we blame for this statistic? Should we blame our genes, what our parents have passed on to us? Or shall we blame our agricultural processes, adulteration of food crops, GM modification, or our ability to cope with that food?

What is an allergic reaction?

When you have an allergy, the immune system elicits an inflammatory response and is usually triggered by the IgE allergens. IgE allergies present as mild such as a runny nose, skin rash, bloating, to as severe as anaphylaxis.

Did you know that your depressed mood, insomnia or aches and pains could be related to diet?

Food intolerances can lead to many health conditions. The most common symptoms of food intolerances are fatigue, bloating or nasal congestion and this may progress to headaches, depression, or aches and pains.

What is the difference between an allergy and an intolerance?

Symptoms of an allergy or an IgE mediated response can range from skin rash to severe anaphylaxis. The response is usually immediate and the symptoms are usually associated with allergen exposure. The conventional RAST test is an IgE or allergy test.

Food intolerances develop over time and measures that innate immunity reflective of gut integrity and enzyme deficiency. Symptoms can vary between bloating, fatigue, flatulence or headaches.

Individuals with neurological, gastrointestinal, and metabolic disorders often suffer from IgG food allergies. These people would continue to eat these foods being unaware of the potential effects. IgG antibodies provide long-term resistance to infections and have a much longer half-life than traditional IgE tests. IgG forms the main antibody component of the blood and interestingly enough, crosses the blood–brain barrier. This is why food intolerances or allergies make us feel rather grumpy and affect mood.

Assessment of food intolerances, sensitivities and allergies

There are two main types of assessments for food allergies. One assesses immunoglobulin (Ig) reaction and another assesses white cell inflammation reaction. An antibody is a protein used by the immune system to identify and neutralise allergens or foreign material like bacteria and viruses. Severe reactions or hypersensitivities are caused by IgE. When the body produces too much of an antibody, it can create a reaction that is represented as intolerance, sensitivity or allergy.

When food is consumed and is not appropriate for the body, the body will react to it as an invader eliciting an allergenic response. The immune system will attack it like it would attack any pathogen to protect the body. This adverse reaction then leads to inflammation often seen in the form of the symptoms associated with food allergies.

Symptoms that may be associated with food sensitivities, intolerances and allergies include:

* **fatigue**
* **dizziness**
* **sinusitis**
* **migraines**
* **itchy skin**
* **anxiety**
* **constipation**
* **diarrhoea**
* **mood disorders**
* **joint pains**
* **sore throat**
* **swelling on tongue or mouth**
* **indigestion**

Immunoglobulin Reactions

Food allergies are immunoglobulin reactions that comes about when food becomes reactive with your body. Allergy to food can lead to tingling on the tongue, swelling around the mouth, asthma, diarrhoea, vomiting choking feeling, or an energy high. Emotional outbursts, irrationality and low mood may also be associated with immunoglobulin reactions.

Allergies elicit IgE mediated reactions leading to inflammation and chronic disease states. The most severe IgE mediated reaction is life threatening anaphylaxis, which requires an immediate adrenaline injection.

IgA pertains to sensitivity and IgG pertains to intolerance of foods.

Secretory IgA (SIgA) is an immune soldier predominantly found in the gut, lungs and mucus membranes. Secretory IgA in the gut protects the body from absorbing food or toxins that are allergenic, and allows this food to be excreted. As we continually expose our body to those very foods that are allergenic to our body, secretory IgA will eventually die down. The SIgA 'soldier' is no longer available to eliminate food allergens allowing for absorption via blood to tissues leading to histamine release, inflammation and allergy.

Foods That Increase Neurotransmitter Production

Neurotransmitters are made from the food we consume. Specific groups of foods have the power to manufacture brain chemicals by the body. Foods that help make dopamine and subsequent adrenal hormones, noradrenaline and adrenaline.

Foods rich in tyrosine and phenylalanine, precursors to dopamine are contained in:

* **fish**
* **eggs**
* **spirulina**
* **beetroot**
* **apples**
* **kale**
* **oregano**
* **bananas**
* **strawberries**
* **green tea**
* **ginkgo biloba**
* **nettles**
* **dandelion**
* **ginseng**

Gingko can also increase dopamine while enhancing oxygen flow and blood flow to the brain.

Exercise stimulates dopamine release. Those who get the 'runners high', floods the brain with 'feel good' hormone called dopamine.

Foods that help make serotonin

Foods rich in tryptophan, the precursor to serotonin are:
* **walnuts**
* **pineapple**
* **bananas**
* **kiwi fruit**
* **plums**
* **tomatoes**
* **eggs**
* **fish**
* **cheese**
* **red meat**
* **poultry**
* **seeds**
* **nuts**
* **soy**
* **oats**
* **chickpeas**

Foods that help make GABA

Food that helps make GABA are also rich in glutamine and glutamate, GABA's precursors.

GABA is created through the process of fermentation. When lactobacillus fermentation conditions are optimal, GABA production by microorganisms is increased. This makes fermented foods like sauerkraut and kimchi, the only dietary source of GABA.

Foods rich in GABA are:
* **wine**
* **green tea and jasmine tea**
* **red meat**

* seafood
* organ meats like liver, brain, kidney
* dairy
* eggs
* nuts
* beans and legumes
* cabbage, beet, spinach, parsley

John's diet adjustments

John's tests revealed severe allergy to peanuts and other seeds, intolerance to grains, dairy and other foods. He adjusted his diet to accommodate the allergies and intolerances. During this time, support of gut integrity with probiotics and prebiotics proved useful. Lactobacills rhamnosus together with a multi strain probiotic improved John's tolerance to foods. After a 3 month abstinence and gut support, he successfully reintroduced foods to which he was previously intolerant.

His neurotransmitter results revealed glutamate toxicity, GABA deficiency and a moderate dopamine depletion.

Foods supporting dopamine production were introduced to his diet.

Foods that are *glutamate* rich are also *glutamine* rich. Glutamate rich foods had become neurotoxic to him. It is essential for John to modify his diet to eliminate neurotoxic foods.

For children with autism and ADHD, they 'seesaw' between glutamate, excitatory neurotransmitter and GABA, the calming agent necessary for speech and concentration.

Too much glutamate causes excitation leading to stimulatory behaviour and excess nerve firing like attention deficit, speech defects and behavioural changes.

When the glutamate/GABA seesaws tips too far over to glutamate, glutamate toxicity results. To keep glutamate levels balanced, it's best to avoid all foods that contain glutamate, glutamic acid, aspartate, aspartic acid and cysteine.

The greatest source of glutamates is mono sodium glutamate (MSG) found in Chinese foods, canned foods, and processed meat.

Excitotoxic foods to avoid:
- **processed noodles**
- **canned foods**
- **processed cheeses**
- **enzyme modified foods**
- **ultra-pasteurised foods**
- **cream and egg substitutes**
- **citric acid from corn**
- **autolysed foods**
- **malted foods**
- **textured proteins**

Does Your Diet Need Adjustment? Take the Quiz!

Do you have a brain chemistry problem?
- *Worry, anxiety*
- *Panic, phobia*
- *Difficulty falling asleep or maintaining sleep*
- *Brain fog, poor focus and memory*
- *Low energy & drive*
- *Negativity, low mood*
- *Sensitivity & emotional*
- *Addictions to food, drugs, alcohol*
- *Overwhelmed, lack of confidence, low self-esteem*

Is your blood sugar in check?
- *Craving sweet things*
- *Craving salty foods*
- *Feel agitated, jittery, irritable*
- *Mental confusion or fogginess*
- *Palpitations*
- *Thirsty*
- *Tired but unable to rest*
- *Hot and bothered*
- *Stressed*
- *Dizzy or weak if a meal is skipped*

Are you allergic to foods?
- *Indigestion*
- *Belching*
- *Bloating*
- *Flatulence or smelly gas*
- *Trouble breathing*
- *Low energy*
- *Irritability*
- *Hyperactivity*
- *Headaches and migraines*

Calculate the number of answers you've circled against the total number of possible results. If you scored more than 30% of the checklist, you may have an imbalance. It is important to investigate your body chemistry with validated functional laboratory testing. (See Chapter 15)

7

The Wired and Tired Brain

When you're cool, calm, and collected and can cope with your daily chores, feel energised and vital, you're free from stress. Stress plays a vital role in mood disorders. In any year around 1 million Australian adults have depression and over two million have anxiety. Many mental health disorders start with stress. Stress is usually the precursor to anxiety, and anxiety is usually the precursor to depression.

When we operate in a realm of fear, anxiety, worry, or stress, we operate within the realms of our *small self*. If we change how we focus our attention, our energy will flow. This is our *bigger self*.

Since stress is the starting point to most mental health disorders, it's important to manage stress simultaneously with balancing neurotransmission pathways. It is cortisol from the adrenals that communicates with the neurotransmitters in the brain which leads to stress, anxiety, depression and other mental health disorders.

Susan's Story

Susan, a 44-year-old female, is a corporate executive known to burn the candles at both ends. She has just broken up with her partner. As her work takes precedence, she has managed a high-functioning workload, social life and exercise routine.

Of late, she feels overwhelmed and exhausted. She has had trouble finding her vehicle in the car park. She even had to return home to check if she locked her door. Focus wanes when the mind is congested. She eats healthily but mostly on the run. She has gained weight particularly around the belly and the hips. She considers herself healthy as she exercises regularly. She used to be a runner. Now she walks and gyms three times a week. When she's under stress she tends to binge eat and enjoys her sweet and salty foods.

She says, 'I feel like I'm running out of gas. I could cope with my workload very easily but can't seem to do so lately.' 'I have an energy slump and tend to crave sweet snacks late afternoon and late at night after dinner. My best work is done in the morning and very late at night. As a result my sleep is disturbed and I don't feel refreshed upon awakening anymore. My brain feels foggy. I'm starting to look old, my skin is starting to dry out and sag.'

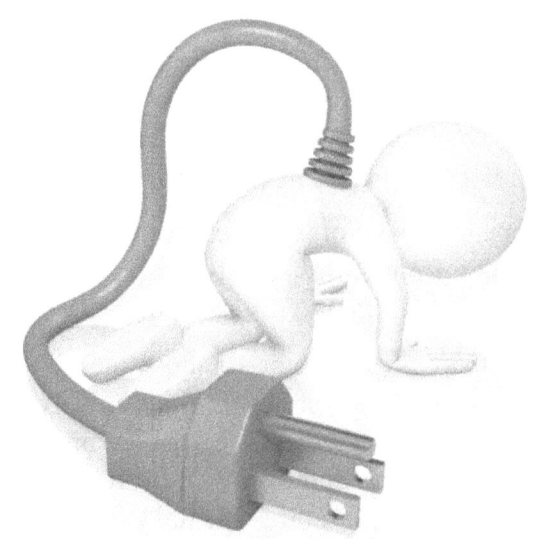

A Sneak Peek at Susan's Adrenal Health

Stress hormones are controlled by the adrenal glands. The adrenal glands sit on top of the kidneys and have two parts, the cortex and the medulla. The adrenal glands secrete cortisol, a stress hormone. Daily secretion of cortisol from the adrenal glands is between 15 to 25 mg per day in females and 25 to 35 mg per day in males.

Cortisol secretion is stimulated during the day by activity or standing. Have you heard of people who complain of feeling dizzy or lightheaded if they stand too quickly? Stress can exacerbate the dizziness or postural hypotension. Cortisol is stimulated by stress and emotions, which everyone can relate to. Cortisol is secreted during bright sunlight especially in the morning. This is why people feel happier when the sun is shining.

Cortisol secretion normally fluctuates throughout the day and night in a circadian rhythm. Cortisol peaks in the morning and depletes through the day, in line with activity and energy.

How Do You Know If Your Adrenals Are Fatigued?

Below is a collection of signs and symptoms that result when the adrenal glands function below the necessary levels. In more serious cases such as in chronic fatigue syndrome, the activity of the adrenal glands is so diminished that patience may have difficulty in getting up out of bed for more than a few hours in a day.

Symptoms of adrenal fatigue may present themselves as the following:
- **tired for no reason**
- **run down or overwhelmed**
- **crave salty and sweet things**
- **have difficulty bouncing back from stress or illness**
- **have trouble getting up in the morning or getting to bed at night**
- **feel more awake and alert after 6 pm than you feel during the day**
- **have a general sense of unwellness, or tiredness**
- **fatigue that is not relieved by sleep**
- **need to use coffee, energy drinks or sweet things to keep you going**

How Common Is Adrenal Fatigue?

About 43% of all adults suffer from stress-related health conditions. More than 70% of all visits to a primary healthcare provider are usually associated with stress related complaints. This accounts for absenteeism from work and if left undertreated, can lead to serious chronic health conditions. Stress is linked to conditions like cardiovascular disease, cancer, lung ailments, guts disturbances and nutritional deficiencies.[20]

Susan said, 'I have a slump in my energy and have gained weight.'

When the adrenals are burnt out, the symptoms one can experience are fatigue, low blood pressure, and sensitivity to light, insomnia, and decreased interest in sex, hypoglycaemia, digestive problems and emotional imbalances.

One man's ability to cope with the same level of stress may differ from another. This may be due to being at different stages of adrenal fatigue.

Three Major Levels of Adrenal Dysfunction

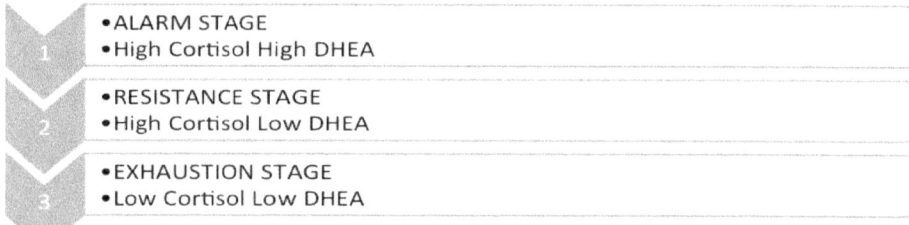

Adrenal sufficiency – when you sit an exam, cortisol levels will rise prior to and during the exam. Once the exam is done, cortisol levels normalise and life goes on. This is a healthy state for the adrenals to be in. Elevations in cortisol are normal in order to get up and go to work or do the chores for the day.

Adrenal insufficiency – you get an abusive phone call, the natural response is to deal with the issue at hand the best you can. You can become red in the face, shaky, agitated or your heart can be pounding during the stress response. When your adrenals are in an insufficient state, cortisol rises and refuses to normalise. This is when you might have a headache or a lump in the throat, develop a cold sweat, heart palpitations, stomach in a knot, constipation, diarrhoea, or muscles start to tighten and weaken. Unfortunately, that stress does not leave you. Instead, you focus on the stress event and worry 24 hours a day, which can cause insomnia and fatigue.

From a spiritual energy perspective, the qi does not flow through the chakras. From the base chakra to the top, the solar plexus will present as 'stomach in a knot', the heart chakra will say 'nobody loves me anymore', the throat chakra will 'think things through over and over again', and the crown chakra will allow stressful thoughts to occupy every waking and sleeping moment.

Cortisol elevation will progressively increase at the expense of other hormones like progesterone and DHEA. Eventually, the hormones DHEA, pregnenalone and progesterone deplete in order to compensate for stress. In the latter phases of adrenal insufficiency, cortisol then starts to deplete leading to the third stage of adrenal dysfunction.[21]

In adrenal exhaustion, typically, you will see a very flat line lower-level of both cortisol and DHEA. There is no energy, the adrenals are starting to shut down. This scenario is typical in a chronic fatigue syndrome or fibromyalgia patient. In severe cases it is likely to see an ambulatory state. It is not unusual to see CFS sufferers bedridden most of the day. This state could be classed as a 'nervous breakdown'.

Why Is Susan Feeling Tired?

Cortisol has many roles in the body. It leaches the calcium out of the bones leading to osteopenia or osteoporotic bones. This is why prolonged stress can contribute towards low bone density, aches and pains, and osteoarthritis. Stress puts an extra load on the heart eventually playing a role in conditions associated with cardiovascular disease, hypercholesterolemia, and inflammatory conditions like diabetes and cancer.

Cortisol suppresses the immune system leading to frequent coughs and colds over time.

Crave salt when stressed? Cortisol alters ATPase enzyme activity in the kidneys. The kidney has many functions including regulating sodium and potassium levels in the blood. An imbalance of sodium can lead to Susan's craving for salty foods. Prolonged sodium and potassium imbalance is associated with high blood pressure.

Cortisol alters synthesis and metabolism of collagen and elastin. This is why chronic stress alters the elasticity, hydration, and thickness of the skin.

Chronic stress uses up more energy in the form of vital nutrients that we get from our food compared to a run around the block. Prolonged stress therefore leads to adrenal fatigue.

Susan is feeling fatigued due to an imbalance of glucose in the body. When the body is undergoing stress, cortisol from the adrenals send signals to the brain to release adrenaline which is what we call the 'adrenaline rush' or 'flight-fright-freeze response'. In order for adrenaline to respond to stress, it requires energy in the form of glucose. Adrenaline will therefore mop up all the glucose that is in the bloodstream for energy to react to the stress. When the glucose is depleted, the brain sends signals to the pancreas to release insulin. Insulin release initiates the need for glucose, hence the need for a 'sugar fix'. The brain however retrieves the energy from glucose stores in muscle and fat tissue. The liver converts glycogen to glucose ready to be used by the brain in response to stress by a process called gluconeogenesis. The quickest source of glucose is a breakdown the muscle.

This is why a stressed person is likely to have muscle aches and pains. In severe instances, lactic acid is released from the muscle tissue leading to lactic acidosis. This could present as the shakes, tremors, or twitching of the muscles. The desperate need for glucose in the form of sugar can eventually lead to increased visceral adiposity and obesity. In rare instances, cortisol may break down adipose fat tissue for energy through a process called glycogenolysis. In these instances, it is common to see weight loss with stress.

Signs and symptoms of low cortisol:
- **adrenal fatigue**
- **allergies**
- **brain fog**
- **chemical sensitivities**
- **sleep disruption**
- **poor immunity**
- **fatigue**
- **flulike symptoms**
- **crave sugars**

Signs and symptoms of high cortisol:
- **ageing**
- **allergies**
- **anxiety**
- **bone loss**
- **dementia**
- **fatigue**
- **high blood pressure**
- **inability to cope with stress**
- **Cushing's syndrome**

Susan has complained of brain fog, poor sleep, lack of focus and attention, and fatigue

These symptoms are signs of low cortisol. She is therefore, likely to be in the latter phase of adrenal insufficiency.

Cortisol works like a seesaw with DHEA, the vitality and youth hormone. As stress goes up, cortisol increases and DHEA decreases. A depletion of DHEA is associated with lack of libido, lack of muscle tone, vitality, mood, bone density, and inflammatory conditions.

How To Measure Stress

Cortisol levels fluctuate through the day. A measure of cortisol in blood or urine once in the morning will only give a snapshot of the levels at the time of collection. An effective way of measuring stress is assessment of cortisol levels at different times in a day. Saliva cortisol testing is effective; saliva is easy to collect and thus cortisol is freely available.

Susan is not sleeping well at night as a result of her prolonged stress

Testing stress in a saliva sample requires collection of a saliva sample four times in a day to best identify imbalances based on diurnal rhythm. In addition, assessment of salivary DHEA, midnight cortisol and melatonin will be appropriate for sleep hormones.

Melatonin is a hormone that is made in the pineal gland found at the base of the brain. Melatonin levels typically deplete as we age, in night shift or airline workers, or through prolonged stress. Melatonin acts as a 'switch on or switch off' trigger that regulates the onset of sleep. If cortisol is elevated at night, stress has the potential to deplete melatonin production which in turn will slow down onset of sleep.

Susan's adrenal fatigue was effectively supported with a blend of adrenal herbs to primarily assist with feeling flat, mental fatigue, physical and nervous exhaustion. Adrenal herbs containing withania, Siberian ginseng, rhodiola, liquorice and amino acid, l-tyrosine was synergistically blended and customised for Susan. Withania, an Ayurvedic herb called ashwaganda, acts as a powerful adrenal supporter by protecting against the negative effects of high cortisol levels found in chronic stress.

Withania acts as a powerful adrenal herb, tonic, anti-inflammatory, and mild sedative used for anxiety, insomnia, and stress associated conditions. Withania is useful for nervous exhaustion and is regarded as a good general tonic for disease prevention.[22]

Siberian ginseng alters the level of hormones involved in stress so that adrenaline and noradrenaline levels are preserved and balanced.[23]

Rhodiola has been shown to improve mental performance in physically stressed and fatigued people. This remarkable herb has a wide and varied history to strengthen the nervous system, assist in the management of depression, enhance immunity, elevate the capacity for exercise, and improve energy levels.[24]

Liquorice has long been used as an adrenal tonic and anti-inflammatory.[25]

Panax ginseng (Korean ginseng) is used both in Chinese and Western herbal medicine as an adaptogenic tonic and immunomodulatory herb.

L-tyrosine is an amino acid that plays an essential role in production of catecholamine neurotransmitters, dopamine, noradrenaline and adrenaline. Tyrosine has been shown to be useful in reducing acute stress, decreasing symptoms associated with cold, stress, hypoxaemia, and improving performance on cognitive skills.[26].

Supplementation with hormone DHEA and cortisone as prescribed by a doctor has been shown to be beneficial for significantly depleted adrenal dysfunction.

Are Your Adrenals in Check?

- *Crave sweet things or carbohydrates*
- *Nervous, irritable, headache, teary*
- *Frequent thirst*
- *Crave salty foods or liquorice*
- *Family history of diabetes, alcoholism*
- *Allergy reactions during seasonal changes*
- *Light-headed, dizzy*
- *Thinking confused when hurried or under pressure*
- *Feeling unwell most of the time*
- *Having to lie down after pressure*
- *Muscles feel weak*
- *Having difficulty getting up in the morning*
- *Suddenly running out of energy*
- *Having an afternoon low*
- *Getting a second burst of energy after dinner*
- *Suffering from allergies*

Calculate the number of answers you've circled against the total number of possible results. If you scored more than 30% of the checklist, you may have an imbalance. It is important to investigate your body chemistry with validated functional laboratory testing. (See Chapter 15)

8

The Sexy Brain

Is Sex All in the Mind?

When sex life is great, the hormones are in balance. When hormones are in balance, you will have a wonderful sexual appetite, and feel healthy, strong and vibrant.

What Does Sex Have to do with Bad Moods?

Sex starts in the mind: feeling, wanting, yearning, touching, and cuddling are all regulated by chemicals in the brain. When sex hormones are out of balance, libido declines significantly. Libido sex hormones influence the brain chemicals directly and can be downregulated pretty quickly under stressful conditions.

Brain Chemicals, Will You Be My Valentine?

Did you know that dopamine may keep the love songs flowing in your relationship?

Dopamine is involved in motivation, pleasure and reward. When dopamine travels along the limbic pathway in the brain, we feel emotions of pleasure and reward. This is why dopamine is called the reward hormone.

Studies using functional MRI scans have shown that dopamine runs rampant when we fall in love. As dopamine is released, intense feelings of pleasure and reward are created. This explains the excitement of new relationships.[27]

Oxytocin - the Cuddle Hormone

Oxytocin is produced in both males and females. Its receptors are found all over the brain and reproductive system. Oxytocin is originally derived from the Greek meaning 'swift birth'. It is used to induce or speed up labour in maternity wards worldwide. Oxytocin is a pro-social hormone that affects the brain as a result of its interactions with gonadal steroids like estrogen, progesterone, testosterone and corticosterone.

The brain affects behaviour, but behaviour also affects the brain. A study found that a whiff of the 'cuddle chemical' oxytocin made men rate their partners as being more attractive.[28]

Oxytocin, which can be found as a nasal spray, is partly responsible for feelings of love and closeness. It is normally released during childbirth to help mothers bond with their babies. Researchers found that a small spray made men's partners more attractive but had no effect on how they perceived strangers or colleagues. *Proceedings of the National Academy of Sciences* stated that the oxytocin released during close physical contact seemed to boost monogamy by making a woman appear more attractive in a man's eyes.

Jane's Story

Jane is a mother of two, 44-years-old, has been suffering with chronic fatigue syndrome. Her life is very busy running an executive job, taxying the children and as a result, struggles to find the time to nurture herself. She falls off to sleep in exhaustion but has trouble maintaining sleep. She feels hot and cold throwing the blankets off regularly through the night causing disturbed sleep. A glass or two of wine tends to assist her stress and improve her sleep patterns. 'I look at myself in the mirror and feel I have aged, my skin is sagging and I'm starting to show wrinkles.' Her husband travels a lot for work and tends to want to rest when he does happen to be home. She finds herself being snappy and making demands on her husband which then affects her marriage. She feels overwhelmed, emotional, forgetful and tired worrying lots. She recalls being efficient at juggling the balls of life.

Her husband has encouraged her to have her hormones checked due to her snappy and irritable demeanour. She had reported that she had gained weight around her belly, hips, upper back and now has defined 'love handles'. Exercise is sporadic these days.. She fires on all cylinders during the day but finds that her energy wanes late afternoon. 'I feel flat, I've lost my libido, my mojo!'

What's Happening to Jane?

As one ages, hormones decline – but they need to decline in balance. When they're out of balance, they create hormonal havoc. Jane presented with low libido. One of the main hormones that is responsible for maintaining libido is testosterone, predominantly a male hormone. All hormones peak at the age of 20 or 30 when we are in the baby boomer or production phase. In a female, hormones fluctuate through a cycle which is usually 28 days. In a normal cycle, oestrogens will peak around ovulation and just before period, whereas progesterone peaks only before the period which is the luteal phase. Even though these hormones deplete as we age, when one hormone depletes out of balance, it leads to dominance of one hormone against the other.

Jane's hormone levels were assessed with a saliva hormone test on day 21 of her cycle (which is mid luteal phase). Her results indicated that she had a low progesterone relative to the oestrogens. Her DHEA and testosterone levels were low normal.

DHEA and testosterone are predominantly male hormones found in smaller quantities in a female body.

What's Happened to Jane's Hormone Levels?

Let's have a sneak peak of how the hormones work. Sex hormones operate much like an orchestra cascading one into the other. The mother hormone is pregnenolone which is metabolised to major hormones, predominantly female hormone called progesterone and predominantly male hormone called DHEA. Note that all of these hormones are found in both males and females in different proportions. Jane's progesterone level was low.

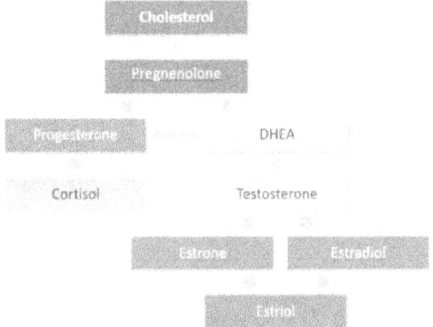

Typical signs and symptoms of low progesterone are:
* disturbed sleep or insomnia
* mood swings
* irritability
* anxiety
* loss of bone density
* pain and inflammation
* decreased HDL

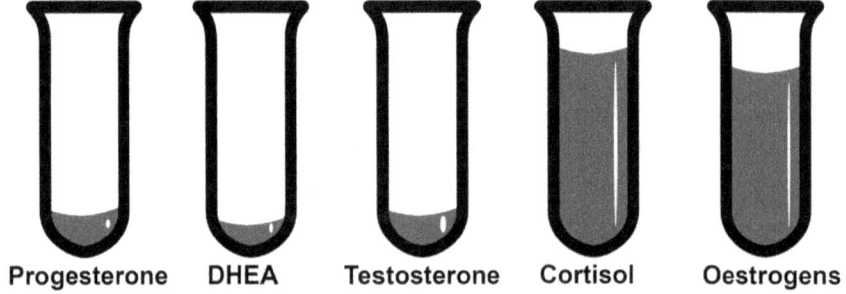

Her total oestrogens were high relative to progesterone leading to what we call oestrogen dominance. Somebody who has oestrogen dominance will feel irritable, moody, hot and bothered, a loss of elasticity of skin, and forgetfulness, and that's the tip of the iceberg.

Oestrogens are necessary in our body to improve sleep, blood flow and insulin sensitivity, regulate body temperature, inhibit platelet stickiness, enhance mood, and decrease wrinkles. Oestrogens also stimulate the production of choline acetyl transferase, an enzyme that prevents Alzheimer's disease.

Oestrogens and progesterone work to balance or oppose each other, a bit of yin and yang. Additionally:
- **Oestrogens retain fluid and cause swelling. Progesterone acts as a diuretic.**
- **Oestrogens increase menstrual flow and proliferation of the endometrium. Progesterone limits endometrial proliferation and limits blood loss.**
- **Oestrogens stimulate the nervous system increasing alertness and nervousness. Progesterone has a calming effect on the body.**

When oestrogens are deficient you may experience hot flushes, night sweats, vaginal dryness, headaches, depression, painful intercourse, low libido, sleep disturbances, bone loss, and foggy thinking.

When oestrogens are in excess, you may experience water retention, breast swelling or tenderness, craving for sweets, fibrocystic breasts, uterine fibroids, fatigue, weight gain, mood swings, low thyroid function, or irregular and heavy menses.

Causes of excess oestrogen in the body may be associated with impaired elimination of oestrogen, taking too much oestrogens, exposure to xeno-oestrogens, lack of exercise, or a diet low in fibre.

Xeno-oestrogens are chemicals that confuse the body because they mimic the natural oestrogens. They occupy the receptor sites for oestrogen blocking oestrogens from functioning normally leading to excess of circulating oestrogens. The human body cannot distinguish between natural oestrogens and xeno-estrogens. These xeno-estrogens accumulate in the body and cause damage, oxidative stress, inflammation, mood changes or may be involved in the development of cancer. Environmental molecules and toxins will compete with endogenous oestrogens for the oestrogen receptor sites. Two major sources of xeno-oestrogens are plastics such as PCB (poly-chlorinated biphenols) and pesticides, especially DDT.

Typical signs and symptoms of excessive oestrogens are:
- **cervical dysplasia**
- **depression with anxiety or agitation**
- **increased risk of uterine cancer**

* **weight gain (abdomen, hips, thighs)**
* **water retention**
* **headaches**
* **poor sleep**
* **panic attacks**
* **swollen breasts**
* **heavy periods**
* **increased risk of breast cancer**
* **increased risk of auto-immune diseases**
* **hypothyroidism**
* **fatigue**
* **irritability/mood swings**
* **uterine fibroids**
* **bloating**

It should be noted that there are three major types of oestrogens in the body made from the male hormone testosterone.

Oestradiol (E2) predominantly controls the heat in the body. Oestradiol is the most important hormone during a female's reproductive years. It is needed by the body for reproduction, maintaining pregnancy, eggs inside a female's ovaries, sexual function, bone health and development of sexual characteristics, improve blood flow and has neuroprotective effects.

Estrogen is thought to activate certain cancer causing genes called oncogenes that raise the risk of breast cancer.

Oestrone (E1) is considered to be the dangerous, proliferative, carcinogenic oestrogen. People who have elevated levels of oestrone require further assessment of its metabolism to 2 and 16-hydroxy oestrogen metabolites. Proliferation of oestrogen receptor positive cells in the body whether it be breast, uterus, endometrium or prostate can lead to conditions like weight gain, irritability, fluid retention, endometriosis, polycystic ovaries, uterine hyperplasia, breast hyperplasia, and benign prostatic hyperplasia in men and if untreated may progress to hormone related cancers both in males and females.

Oestriol (E3) is manufactured from both conversion of E2 and E1. This is the most abundant, safe oestrogen in the body. As we age, mucus membranes thin out.

Women who suffer from dry vagina or vaginal atrophy would benefit from oestriol supplementation.

A deficiency of oestrogens are associated with:
- **hot flushes and night sweats**
- **emotional, confused, depression, irritability**
- **lack of motivation, restlessness**
- **fatigue**
- **lack of libido, diminished orgasm**
- **urinary incontinence**
- **vaginal dryness**
- **painful intercourse**
- **insomnia, difficulty falling asleep**
- **headaches**
- **joint and back pain**
- **weight gain**
- **changes in memory & focus**
- **risk of heart disease**

Jane's DHEA and testosterone levels were low normal

These are androgens (or male hormones) found in both males and females. DHEA is considered to be the youthful hormone. DHEA depletion leads to a lack of vitality, bone density, strength muscle, memory and focus.

DHEA, the youthful hormone, makes testosterone and androstenedione, and more male hormones.

Testosterone, like DHEA is responsible for libido, vital function, muscle strength, and memory. Signs and symptoms of testosterone depletion are muscle wasting, weight gain, low self-esteem, decreased HDL, dry thin skin, thinning hair, droopy eyelids, sagging cheeks, and adrenal fatigue.

Have you ever felt totally irrational and aggressive one minute and perfectly normal, calm and collected the next? Fluctuations in testosterone levels can cause these emotional outbursts. Some women who have high levels of testosterone relative to DHEA might feel like a 'teenager recycled', with facial hair growth, hair loss on the scalp or acne as in their teenage years, salt and sugar cravings, insulin resistance, hypoglycaemia, and increased risk of heart disease.

What Have Sex Hormones Got to do with the Brain?

A lack of testosterone is associated with low libido. Testosterone is made from DHEA, a hormone that works in balance with the stress hormone, cortisol. There is no point adding testosterone into her hormone mix unless the adrenals are managed at the same time. When the adrenals are managed, DHEA and cortisol are in balance, testosterone has the potential to normalise.

Jane said, 'I am feeling overwhelmed and the smallest tasks are a big deal for me. My libido is low.'

Feelings of being overwhelmed are associated with adrenal fatigue and stress. Stress hormones responsible for regulating adrenals are cortisol and DHEA. They perform like a seesaw. If stress is high, cortisol will rise and DHEA will dip. This is why Jane has cravings for sweet things in the afternoon because her cortisol is stealing from all the other hormones to compensate and manage the stress. The body's response to stress will always override hormone function.

Pregnenolone makes DHEA and progesterone, and progesterone makes cortisol. If stress is high, cortisol rises at the cost of depletion in progesterone, pregnenolone and DHEA.

Jane's adrenal hormones were supported with specific herbs like withania, rhodiola and ginseng. For her libido, herbs have been shown to effectively support testosterone and regulate sexual function.

Herbs such as tribulis and damiana have been shown to increase androgen levels which influence nitric oxide in the brain. Nitric oxide is a vasodilator that may enhance sexual desire and libido.

Damiana supports sexual desire by increasing dopamine tone and indirectly supports oxytocin release. Lotus seed, an Ayurvedic herb, has been shown to increase arousal and intensify sexual desire.

Jane said, 'I am feeling low, not at all happy.'

Stress plays a major role in depression. Jane is feeling low as her stress hormone is driving her happy hormone – serotonin – down.

Excess cortisol, the stress hormone can block serotonin synthesis and the metabolism of serotonin leading to depression. This is why Jane is feeling low.

Cortisol deficiency, on the other hand, decreases serotonin and adrenaline but increases noradrenaline and glutamate levels. If glutamate and noradrenaline levels peak, you may experience aggression, irrationality and anxiety.

Jane said that she is craving certain foods particularly salty and sweet things late afternoon.

Elevated cortisol will alter sodium and potassium levels in the bloodstream. A depletion of potassium is associated with mood changes. Sodium and potassium need to be in balance to maintain kidney function and blood pressure. This is why Jane is craving salty things.

Elevated cortisol will stimulate adrenergic response in line with the flight-fright-freeze adrenaline rush. The need for food in the form of glucose or sugar to support the adrenaline rush will eventually deplete blood glucose, which, in turn will trigger the craving for sugar.

Jane said, 'I feel flat, I've lost my mojo.'

Jane's test results indicated a low level of DHEA, the youthful and vital hormone. DHEA enhances dopamine, noradrenaline and serotonin. DHEA has the capacity to be neuroprotective and increase neuronal plasticity.

Low DHEA levels are contributing to lack of vitality, and lack of adrenal reserve.

Jane said, 'I am hot and bothered and can't sleep at night. A glass or two of wine helps me sleep better.'

Both progesterone and oestrogen may be both depleted; when progesterone is depleted relative to oestrogen, it can lead to a condition called oestrogen dominance. Oestrogens need to be in balance within the body. Oestrogens are metabolised by glucoronidation, a liver detoxification pathway. When the liver is not functioning effectively or detoxifying effectively, oestrogens accumulate. Conditions under which the liver does not detoxify effectively are excess toxicity, too much alcohol consumption, pharmaceutical drugs and poor metabolism. One of the main cofactors necessary for detoxification of oestrogens is calcium-D-glucarate.

Jane's test results indicated low progesterone. Progesterone as well as alcohol are GABA stimulators. GABA is a mood balancer and without it, we cannot relax and feel anxious. Low-levels of progesterone will be one of the contributing factors to hot flushes. Low progesterone will drive down GABA which contributes to the panic and anxiety she is experiencing.

Progesterone production multiplies tenfold when a woman first becomes pregnant. This is why pregnant women in the first trimester feel calm and relaxed and could probably sleep all day. That's the progesterone-GABA hit.

Progesterone should not be confused with progestins, or synthetic progestogen – for example, medroxy progesterone acetate, a pharmaceutical drug.

Natural progesterone is the same molecule that our body naturally synthesises; this is molecularly and structurally identical to that which the body makes, hence the term 'bioidentical'.

Progesterone has many functions, which differ from the synthetic version.

Bioidentical progesterone:
- **helps balance oestrogen**
- **improves sleep**
- **is a calming hormone**
- **lowers elevated blood pressure**
- **lowers cholesterol**
- **is a natural diuretic**
- **is a natural antidepressant**
- **increases scalp hair**
- **protects against breast cancer**
- **helps balance fluid in the cells**

Jane said, 'My skin is sagging I am feeling hot and bothered.'

The production of oestrogen declines with age. Oestrogen receptor sites are found predominantly in sex organs such as breast, uterus, and ovaries but also in the skin. Oestrogens play a vital role in protection of skin ageing by increasing skin thickness, retaining moisture. Oestrogens increase the synthesis of collagen, the skin's underlying support structure to maintain skin youthfulness Collagen atrophy and dehydration are major problems in skin ageing. There is a strong correlation between collagen loss and oestrogen deficiency during menopause. Calleja-Agius J, Muscat-Baron Y, Brincat MP. Skin ageing. *Menopause Int.* 2007 Jun;13(2): 60–4.

Natural Treatment Strategies for Jane

Jane's hormonal levels were balanced with a treatment of specific herbs to boost progesterone, cleared the excess oestrogens from her body with oestrogen modulators, a liver detoxification program, and supported her DHEA and testosterone levels.

Progesterone boosting herbs and nutrients used were vitex, perilla, parsley, quercetin, vitamin D, B6, B3, B2, B5 and vitamin A.

Vitex is used to regulate menstrual cycle, assist in the management of PMS symptoms such as breast tenderness, tiredness, moodiness, headaches, bloating and fluid retention and assist in management of hot flushes and healthy hormone metabolism.

Vitamin B6 helps to relieve hormonal imbalance via its action as a cofactor for several neurotransmitters involved in mood regulation.

Vitex relieves hormonal symptoms by binding to dopamine receptors and inhibiting prolactin. High levels of prolactin may inhibit corpus luteal development, thereby reducing the secretion of progesterone in the luteal phase of the menstrual cycle.[29]

A prescription of DHEA supplementation was used for 3 months to stimulate DHEA and testosterone production and drive down elevated cortisol. DHEA gave her vitality and allowed her to cope with stress, and helped her to feel less overwhelmed and improved her libido. Her doctor was keen to supplement her hormones for a limited time frame to meet her physiological needs and not shut down her endogenous production.

She was prescribed an antiaging facial skin cream containing oestrogen. She reported that her hormone cream was the face lift she needed. Her skin looked well hydrated, her skin texture improved and the sagging was starting to lift.

She said, 'I have actually slept through the night. I don't feel hot and bothered anymore. I'm getting my mojo back slowly. The kids have noticed that I'm not as irritable and snappy. Mum is actually laughing at our jokes. Guess what? I actually feel like being intimate again.'

What's good for the goose, is good for the gander! *Peter, Jane's husband observed the changes in his wife and chose to take the plunge of having his hormone levels tested.*

Peter's Story

Peter, Jane's husband, travels for work eating convenient fast foods of many cuisines.

He's been struggling of late with fatigue, indigestion, bloating, and a decreased desire for sex. His bowel habits can fluctuate from constipation to diarrhoea. He notices that he has loose stools when he travels

He has developed a potbelly, his hair has started to recede, erections are shorter and he seems to snap at his colleagues. Peter has noticed that he needs to urinate more often, and feels as if he has not completely emptied his bladder.

As a man ages, his hormone levels, particularly DHEA and testosterone decline leading to a condition called andropause or more recently ADAM (androgen deficiency in the ageing male). DHEA is a hormone made by the adrenal glands, the brain, and the skin. Its production declines as we age. By the age of 70, the male body may only make a quarter of the amount of DHEA. DHEA is a precursor hormone to progesterone testosterone and testosterone is the precursor to all the oestrogens.

Typical signs and symptoms of ADAM are:
- **low libido**
- **erectile dysfunction**
- **weight gain**

* low stamina
* irritability
* loss of skin elasticity
* decreasing muscle mass
* stiffness and pain in muscles and joints
* increase in body fat
* increase in wrinkles

How Hormones Work in a Male

DHEA converts to testosterone. Testosterone undergoes one of two pathways to convert either to oestrogens or dihydrotesterone (DHT).

Oestrogen excess in a male can lead to enlarged prostate, leading to benign prostatic hyperplasia (BPH), urine retention, urine urgency, stress incontinence, impotence, low sex drive, depression, and increasing weight.

Factors that increase ageing in a male or testosterone to oestrogen conversion via aromatase activity are:
* impaired liver function
* zinc deficiency
* overuse of alcohol
* drug-induced oestrogen imbalance
* exposure to xeno-oestrogens
* obesity

Symptoms associated with testosterone and DHT deficiency are:
* hair loss
* pale skin
* small wrinkles around the eyes and mouth
* poor moustache and beard growth
* muscle flaccidity
* gynaecomastia (or 'man boobs')
* flabby belly
* poor mental strength, anxiety, emotional
* low physical endurance
* poor libido and sexual potency

A depletion of DHT is associated with benign prostatic hyperplasia (BPH), urine retention, urine urgency, stress incontinence, hair loss and thinning of body hair.

Peter Complained of Increased Frequency of Urination and Receding Hairline

Elevated levels of oestrone is associated with oestrogen receptor positive proliferation of the prostate gland. Benign prostatic hyperplasia (BPH) is associated with elevated levels of oestrone. In addition, Peter has been "short" with his colleagues. Men become grumpy and irritable as testosterone converts to the oestrogens, much like a woman in menopause.

Abnormalities in conversion of testosterone to DHT is not only associated with BPH, but also hair loss typically seen as a receding hair line. Peter has reported hair loss.

Pharmaceutical medication works at inhibiting both aromatase and 5-alpha reductase to assist with hair loss and BPH.

Natural Treatment Strategies

Peter's saliva test measured for pertinent hormones, DHEA, testosterone, androstenedione, oestrone and oestradiol. He was quite relieved that it took a simple DIY saliva sample to offer clues to his low libido.

His results reported low normal levels of DHEA, normal testosterone, low DHT, normal E2 and a high E1.

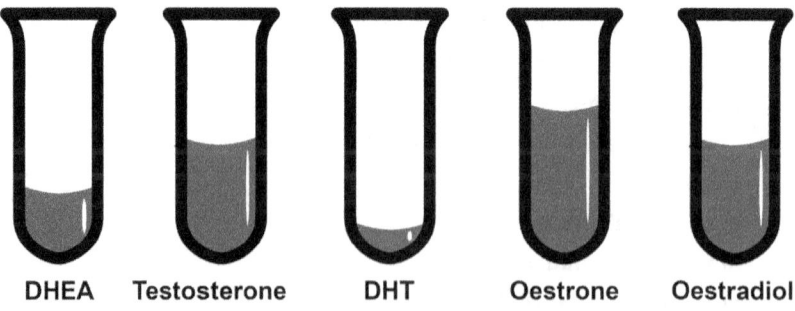

Peter's diet was structured to eliminate processed foods and eat healthily with fresh, wholesome and organic foods. A change in diet allowed him to feel more energised, less bloated and regular in his bowel habits.

Peter started a tailored blend of herbs and vitamins to support aromatase and 5-alpha reductase enzymes to optimise his hormonal status. The blend of herbs contained tribulus, saw palmetto, nettle, Japanese knotwood, damiana and withania.[30]

Saw palmetto is used primarily to manage benign prostatic hyperplasia (BPH), as an inhibitor of 5-alpha reductase. In other words saw palmetto inhibits the conversion of testosterone to DHT thereby increasing the levels of DHT.[31]

Lower levels of DHT are associated with hair loss and BPH. Men with BPH have increased urine frequency, nocturnal urination, decreased urine flow, urine hesitation, irritation and dribbling with incomplete emptying of the bladder.

Vitamins and minerals like zinc, sesame, brassica, riboflavin, nicotinamide, zinc, selenium were given to support hormone synthesis and regulation.[32]

When the male hormones are in check and optimised, libido restores, 'man boobs' recede, hair becomes luscious, and erectile function restores to youthful levels.

Hormones in Check? Take the Quiz!

For females:

PMS
- *Insomnia*
- *Breast tenderness*
- *Abdominal bloating*
- *Depressed, irritable*
- *Fluid retention*
- *Food cravings*
- *Oily skin*
- *Headaches*

- ◊ Back pain
- ◊ Uterine cramping

Menopause

- ◊ Irregular menstrual cycle
- ◊ Disinterest in sex
- ◊ Depression, anxiety
- ◊ Stress
- ◊ Dry skin
- ◊ Dry vagina
- ◊ Night sweats
- ◊ Back pain
- ◊ Crave sweet things
- ◊ Hot flushes
- ◊ Poor memory
- ◊ Bloating
- ◊ Loss of skin elasticity

Progesterone imbalance

- ◊ Anxiety
- ◊ Lumpy breasts
- ◊ Weight gain
- ◊ Disturbed sleep
- ◊ Poor memory
- ◊ Hair growth on body
- ◊ Bloating
- ◊ Headaches
- ◊ Low sex drive

Oestrogen imbalance

- ◊ Vaginal dryness
- ◊ Poor memory
- ◊ Vaginal dryness
- ◊ Irritability
- ◊ Lethargy
- ◊ Night sweats

For males:
- *Fatigue*
- *Depression, feel flat*
- *Erectile dysfunction*
- *Low libido*
- *Loss of early morning erection*
- *Pot belly*
- *Dry skin*
- *Dripping after urination*
- *Interrupted urine flow*
- *Sense of bladder fullness*
- *Irritability, grumpy*
- *Muscle and joint aches*
- *Decreased muscle mass*

Calculate the number of answers you've circled against the total number of possible results. If you scored more than 30% of the checklist, you may have an imbalance. It is important to investigate your body chemistry with validated functional laboratory testing. (See Chapter 15)

9

The Thermostat Brain

The brains thermostat is governed by the thyroid gland which lives in the throat wrapped around the trachea. This organ's job is to maintain temperature or thermogenesis and metabolism. People with thyroid disorders often have emotional or mental health symptoms. If you're experiencing low moods, feeling flat or slow in your activity or thinking, you may have an underactive thyroid. Hypothyroidism or low thyroid function is associated with depression, low mood, mood swings and sleeping difficulties. Conversely, a person with an overactive thyroid seen in hyperthyroidism might experience emotional anxiety, a feeling of nervousness, a racing heart and trembling.

When thyroid function is optimal, you will feel energised, have a great metabolism and regulate body temperature naturally. Most will not recognise thyroid imbalances until symptoms present in line with testing as thyroid symptoms may be masked by other conditions like fatigue or mood changes.

Faye's Story

Faye, a 44-year-old female, is sick and tired of being told that she is depressed. She presented to the doctors with low mood, feeling flat, lack of motivation, and fatigue. She feels flat all day. She needs to drag herself to do her daily chores and get to work. Her mum has Hashimoto's thyroiditis which is managed with thyroid medication. She constantly feels cold in the bones, and particularly cold hands and feet. Her doctor had measured her thyroid, which was reported as being normal. She was then given an SSRI to support her moods. She had become convinced that she had a mental health disorder and resigned herself to taking antidepressant prescription medication long-term. The antidepressant had not made any significant difference to her moods. Fay said, 'I just feel flat, I feel stressed and tired all the time.'

What's Happened to Faye's Thyroid Function?

A report from Faye's doctor indicated that her thyroid function was normal. After examination of her test results, it was determined that TSH was measured as a mark of thyroid function. Her TSH was 4.2 U/ml with a reference of 0.5 to 5 U/ml. For optimal thyroid function TSH should ideally be between 1 U/ml and 2 U/ml. Anything beyond the optimal range but within the normal reference range would be associated with a subclinical thyroid dysfunction. Faye's TSH levels above 2 U/ml but below 5 U/ml is indicative of subclinical or functional hypothyroidism. The most observable sign of hypothyroidism is a low basal body temperature upon awakening in the morning. Faye always felt cold. As Faye has typical signs and symptoms of low thyroid function, it is important to identify her thyroid hormones and thyroid antibodies.

There is a possibility that Faye could develop Hashimoto's thyroiditis because of the genetic predisposition in the family.

Is Stress Linked to Thyroid?

Stress and fatigue are signs of adrenal dysfunction. The hypothalamus, pituitary and adrenals are intimately related to hypothalamus, pituitary and thyroid function. If you have adrenal dysfunction, or experience chronic stress, this could lead to adrenal insufficiency and fatigue, and the adrenal dysfunction contributes toward slowing the thyroid down. Someone who is adrenal insufficient does not always have thyroid dysfunction but there is a great tendency to slowing thyroid function. On the other hand, a person with thyroid dysfunction should always support adrenal function in line with managing the thyroid.

High stress, which is associated with high cortisol levels, can inhibit the production of TSH in the pituitary gland and decrease thyroid receptor site activity by more than 50%.

Hypothyroidism is common in women aged between 35 and 60. About 20% of women over the age of 60 are affected by subclinical hypothyroidism. By the age of 65, 17% of women have hypothyroidism compared to 9% of men.

Adrenal dysfunction shares many symptoms with the low thyroid. The main differentiating criteria in thyroid is that the body temperature will be low with very little variability, and energy will be flat-lined low throughout the day. In an adrenal dysfunction the temperature variability is high and energy may fluctuate at different times of the day.

In hypothyroidism, you might:
* **suffer fatigue all day**
* **feel the same emotion all day**
* **have a preference for sugar and caffeine**

In adrenal fatigue, you might:
* **feel fatigue early morning and mid afternoon**
* **feel worse in the morning and have a second wind of energy at night**
* **prefer fats and proteins with caffeine**

Prolonged stress is usually associated with elevated cortisol which has the potential to inhibit thyroid hormone production. Cortisol is needed for T3 affinity to the thyroid hormone receptor sites. High cortisol levels can inhibit the de-iodination, an enzymatic process of conversion of T4 to T3.

There are many links between depression, hypothyroidism and hyperthyroidism.

Digging Deeper into Thyroid Hormones

Thyroid stimulating hormone (TSH) is the key signal to make thyroid hormones. When the circulating thyroid hormones are low, the pituitary gland releases thyroid stimulating hormone. As thyroid hormones increase, TSH production decreases, which in turn slows the release of new hormones from the thyroid gland. The two primary hormones that control the thyroid are thyroxine (T4) ,a hormone that is predominantly inactive and prescribed as thyroxine for thyroid hormone replacement therapy. T4 is die-iodinated to be converted to an active triiodothyronine (T3) which signals the body to produce energy in the form of adenosine triphosphate (ATP). T3 allows the body to boost metabolic energy production when it is needed. About 80% of T3 is made from T4 in the thyroid liver and kidneys.

Under stressful conditions, T4 cannot effectively convert to T3, and instead T4 converts to reverse T3 (rT3). Reverse T3 is made by the body to regulate T3 energy production by removing a different iodine from T4. Reverse T3 blocks T3 from signalling cells to make energy. Instead, it turns down energy when it is needed. High levels of reverse T3 will therefore slow thyroid function. Stress therefore slows production of active T3 but increases damaging reverse T3 levels.

The Key Players in Thyroid Function

The activity of thyroid gland is regulated by the level of iodine available and through negative feedback systems involving the hypothalamus and pituitary gland. Synthesis of thyroid hormones takes place in the follicles of the thyroid gland and is dependent on the presence of two key nutrients, namely iodine and tyrosine. Iodide must undergo oxidation to iodine in order to bind to tyrosine. Thyroid releasing hormone (TRH) is produced by the hypothalamus to regulate TSH release by the pituitary.

TSH stimulates the growth and activity of the thyroid follicle cells and releases T4 and T3.

T4 is a predominantly inactive pro hormone produced mainly in the liver, kidney and muscles.

T3 is the active form of thyroid hormone affecting metabolism and energy production.

Key cofactors required to convert T4 to an active T3 are iodine, selenium, an amino acid called tyrosine, zinc and antioxidants. Interestingly, tyrosine is also required to synthesise a neurotransmitter called dopamine. Someone who has low thyroid function is likely to have a low dopamine and subsequent low mood.

Factors that may inhibit active thyroid hormone synthesis
* **deficiency of the cofactors like selenium and zinc**
* **chronic stress**
* **toxicity of cadmium as seen in smoking, mercury or lead toxicity**
* **inadequate nutrition, protein or starvation**
* **high carbohydrate diet**
* **decreased liver or hepatic function**
* **decreased renal function**

Anti-thyroglobulin antibodies (ATG Ab) is a thyroglobulin protein from which T3 and T4 produced.

Thyroid peroxidase antibodies (TPO Ab) are responsible for iodination and utilisation of tyrosine in the thyroglobulin molecule.

TSH receptor antibodies (TSH Rec Ab) can mimic the action of TSH and cause hypothyroidism, Graves' disease can antagonise TSH and cause hypothyroidism.

The presence of elevated thyroid antibodies is indicative of autoimmune disease of the thyroid. The most common autoimmune thyroid dysfunction is Hashimoto's thyroiditis, then Graves' disease, or postpartum thyroiditis.

In Hashimoto's thyroiditis, which is a hypothyroidism auto-immune condition, an infiltration of lymphocytes leads to inflammation and wasting of the thyroid gland.

Thyroid and Mood

Due to the close association of thyroid and adrenals, the incidence of depression and anxiety is 2.3 times higher with subclinical hypothyroidism as opposed to euthyroid patients.[33]

Thyroid hormones are widely distributed in the brain and have shown to increase serotonin transmission by changing the sensitivity of serotonin receptors, causing an overall increase in serotonin activity. This is how balancing thyroid hormones can assist in alleviation of depression.[34]

Serotonin modulates thyroid function. The diurnal rhythms of TSH production are dependent upon serotonin. 5-hydroxy tryptophan, the precursor of serotonin has been shown to elevate TSH levels.[35]

Excess GABA can impede thyroid function. Thyroid hormones interact with dopamine predominantly on the basis of the fact that its precursor amino acid, tyrosine, is needed for optimal thyroid function and production of dopamine. Dopamine deficiency increases thyroid stimulating hormone (TSH).[36]

In light of the close association between thyroid dysfunction and mood disorders, the diagnosis of subclinical or clinical hypothyroidism must be considered in patients with depression. Note that the vast majority of depressed patients may have biochemical evidence of normal thyroid function.

Symptoms of low or high functioning thyroid and depression share many commonalities, therefore can be masked as depression instead of a thyroid dysfunction.

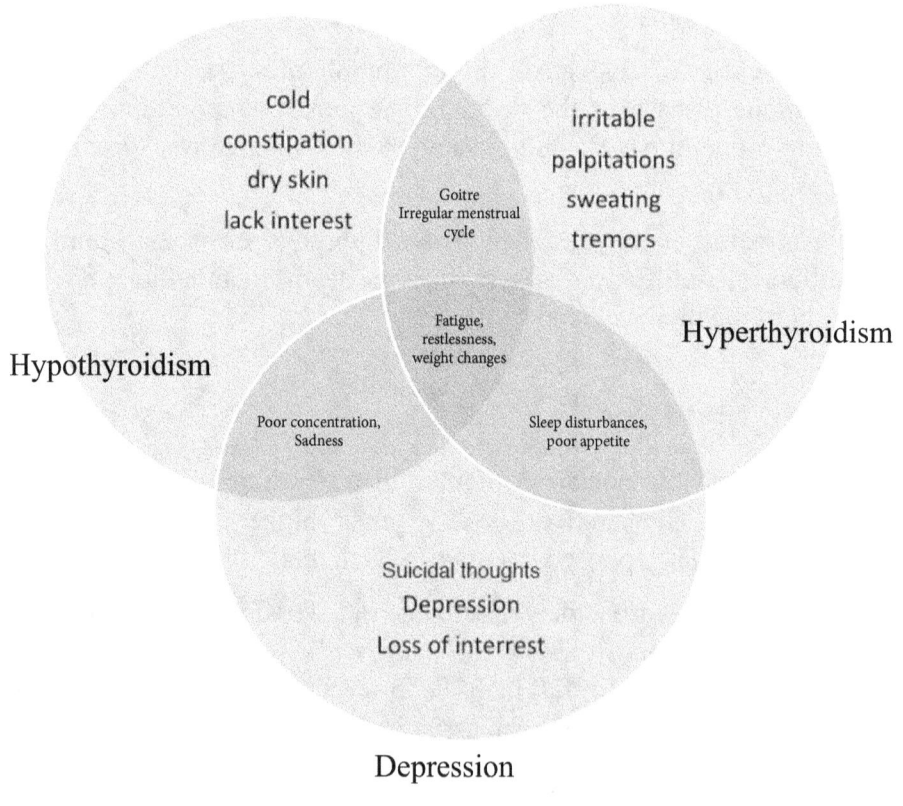

Testing the Thyroid

The key to testing thyroid is to determine the amount of active T3 thyroid hormone. TSH measure is not enough. Hypothyroid patients on thyroxine (T4) may still feel tired and moody. T4 supplementation may not be sufficient, therefore enhance production of T3.

The ideal thyroid test would measure TSH, T3, T4, reverse T3, iodine, tyrosine, selenium and all thyroid antibodies.

Faye said, 'I feel the cold in my bones.'

Faye had charted her temperature for 5 consecutive days to confirm a possible thyroid dysfunction. Temperature charting is probably the oldest telltale sign of thyroid dysfunction. Body temperatures below 36.4°C indicate a low thyroid. Temperature fluctuations can vary between an adrenal and thyroid deficiency. In adrenal fatigue, temperature may fluctuate up and down with high variability in line with fluctuating energy. In thyroid dysfunction, temperature may be consistently low in line with low energy throughout the day.

A household thyroid test, one which is not scientifically validated, involves application of one drop of Lugol's iodine to the inner wrist. If the iodine stain disappears within hours, the body has absorbed the iodine indicating the need for iodine in order for the thyroid to operate effectively. If the stain remains and has not changed markedly, the body may be iodine sufficient.

Faye's Thyroid Treatment Strategies

Faye's thyroid test results revealed a high normal TSH, normal T4 and low normal T3. Elevated TSH is an indicator for further thyroid hormone assessments. Her thyroid antibodies were normal. Good news as she was concerned that she may have been genetically susceptible to Hashimoto's thyroiditis, which her mother suffers from.

Faye reported that her basal body temperature was low after temperature charting for 5 days. Her doctor did not prescribe thyroid medication for her. He advised that he would monitor her levels over the next 6 months.

Supplementation consisted of adrenal and thyroid support with herbs,

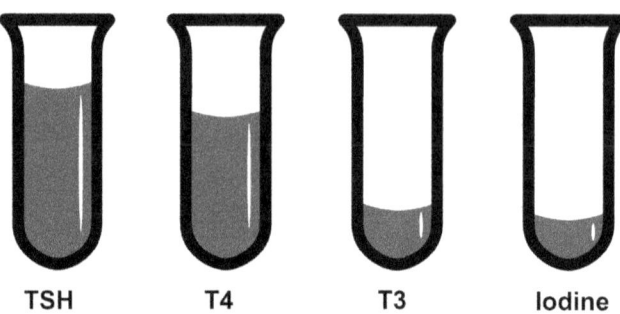

vitamins and antioxidants. Treatment used to support adrenal and thyroid function contained in a supplement with withania, rhodiola, coleus together with tyrosine, vitamin A, vitamin C, vitamin D, zinc, quercetin, selenium and iodine.

Faye reported an improvement in energy, motivation, and mood within days. Over time, her temperature intolerance ceased to become an issue. Within a few months, she was ready to discuss cessation of her antidepressant medication with the doctor.

It is essential to use prescription medication to manage the thyroid if recommended. Conventionally, thyroxine (T4), compounded thyroid extract (also known as Armour Thyroid), levothyronine (T3) and thyroid glandulars are prescribed for hypothyroidism and neomercazole for hyperthyroidism.

Always correct the physiological and biochemical imbalances by replenishing the cofactors that are required to manufacture active thyroid hormone.

Treatment strategies for hypothyroidism aim to:
* **support healthy thyroid function**
* **assist in normal synthesis and activation of thyroid hormones**
* **support healthy liver metabolism and detoxification**
* **provide antioxidant support**
* **assist in reduction of symptoms associated with the hypothyroidism**

Some of the relevant treatment strategies include but not conclusive are:
* **Iodine, selenium, zinc, and vitamin E, which play a significant role in the synthesis and the regulation of thyroid hormones. Zinc and vitamin E also provide antioxidant activity by restricting free radical damage.**

* Zinc plays a key role in thyroid function by enhancing thyrotropin releasing hormone (TRH) synthesis and conversion of T4 to T3.[37]
* Quercetin is a powerful antioxidant, anti-inflammatory agent used to support thyroid function especially in the treatment of Graves' disease.[38]
* Tyrosine makes dopamine to improve mood and cognition, and makes the thyroid work. Low levels of amino acid, tyrosine has been associated with a decreased level of T4 and T3. Tyrosine is found in many high protein foods such as chicken, turkey, fish, peanuts, avocados, cheese, milk, lima beans, pumpkin seeds and cottage cheese.[39]
* Withania is one of the most powerful adaptogenic Indian herbs which has been shown to increase T3 by 18% and T4 by 111%. Withania acts as a GABA mimetic to relieve anxiety.[40]
* Lemon balm blocks TSH and TSH-receptor antibody binding to TSH receptor, thereby disrupting thyroid signalling. Lemon balm is useful in management of Graves' disease and anxiety.[41]
* Coleus, an Indian herb also known as forskolin, has been shown to have similarly effects to TSH, producing an eightfold increase in the secretion of thyroid hormones. Bone K.[42]
* Prunella is a traditional Chinese medicine used as an antioxidant and anti-inflammatory by clearing heat associated with thyroid nodules like goitre.[43]
* Rehmannia also known as Chinese foxglove is used synergistically with other herbs for conditions that feature heat and irritability.
* Phyllanthis embelica also known as Indian gooseberry is a cooling herb used in reducing oxidative stress

Natural treatment strategies for hypothyroidism:
* key minerals, namely iodine selenium and zinc
* amino acids such as tyrosine, cysteine, methionine and taurine
* vitamins A, C, D and E
* herbs such as bupleurum, withania, rhodiola and coleus

Vitamin C and selenium are needed as catalysts for thyroid hormone production.

An amino acid or protein deficient diet particularly cysteine deficiency may reduce the turnover of T4 to T3.[44]

Iodine is an essential element for the production of thyroid hormones. Iodine deficiency is common in many areas of the world and is the main cause of goitre, seen as a generalised enlargement of the thyroid gland. The World Health Organisation recommends a range of 152 to 49 ug/l during pregnancy. Supplementation of iodine is required in hypothyroidism as well as fibrocystic breast disease.[45]

Is Your Thyroid in Check? Take the Quiz!

Signs and symptoms of hypothyroidism or low thyroid function:
- *fatigue*
- *constipation*
- *weight gain*
- *intolerance to cold*
- *dry skin or hair*
- *depression*
- *poor concentration*
- *memory impairment, apathy*
- *muscle aches and pains, cramps*
- *slow heartbeat*
- *irregular or heavy periods*
- *fluid retention*

Signs and symptoms of hyperthyroidism or overactive thyroid:
- *fatigue*
- *palpitations*
- *high blood pressure*
- *weight loss*
- *poor concentration*
- *anxiety and restlessness*
- *irritability*
- *muscle weakness*
- *heating tolerance*
- *increased weight*
- *frequent bowel movements*
- *irregular periods*

Calculate the number of answers you've circled against the total number of possible results. If you scored more than 30% of the checklist, you may have an imbalance. It is important to investigate your body chemistry with validated functional laboratory testing. (See Chapter 15)

10

The Fat and Frumpy Brain

Ever wondered why you eat less and still gain weight? Isn't it frustrating when you're doing the best you can with your diet and continue to expand into a pear or apple shape.

In the ideal world, we would like to be trim, taut and terrific both on the inside and the outside.

There's a significant correlation between depression and being fat and frumpy. One of the documented side effects of SSRIs is weight gain which may be hard to shake off even after getting off antidepressants. Neurotransmitters, important neuropeptides, and the brain's appetite regulatory complex all control appetite, satiety and cravings.

Sita's Story

Sita, a 38-year-old mother of one, has expanded in the hips and tummy particularly in the last year. She has gained weight in the back, under the arms, under the boobs and developed a belly fat pad. She finds it hard to exercise regularly as she works full-time and is exhausted at the end of each day. She walks her dog for half an hour two to three times per week and does one gym class per week. Her muscles seem to ache upon exertion. She believes that her life is no more stressful than any other mum and worker. She finds it a challenge to keep up with her social life or do any additional study. Her brain feels rather foggy these days. Sita said, 'I have brain drain, my diet is healthy, but I do love my sweets after dinner'. She has a family history of diabetes. Her test results revealed a marginally elevated glucose.

The Obesity Epidemic

Obesity has reached epidemic proportions worldwide leading to complex and chronic health conditions. WHO (World Health Organisation) have reported the statistic for obesity is 2.3 billion worldwide. Ten years ago, the world had 1.6 billion overweight adults.

Obesity is not only associated with diet, lifestyle and exercise, but also genetic makeup. Perhaps we can blame the high calorie intake, high sugar or the agricultural processes. Obesity is essentially high body fat relative to lean body mass. Traditionally, body mass index, which is a relationship of weight and height, was considered the gold standard to determine the level of obesity. A BMI over 30 is considered obese.

Review the diet if you happen to feel fatigued, have a woolly head or have disturbed gastrointestinal symptoms. It is the diet that produces energy through the metabolic processes in the body. Any kinks in energy production will create metabolic blocks in the conversion of food to energy.

The process of energy production in the body is called the Krebs cycle. Fats, carbohydrates, and protein from the diet are processed through the gastrointestinal tract to produce nutrients that are transported via the bloodstream or the portal system to the liver. The liver is responsible for detoxification of all nutrients which are will be taken up by the mitochondria or within each cell in the body to produce energy in the form of ATP (adenosine triphosphate). Very important essential nutrients and amino acids are required to stimulate production of ATP. Elevations of organic acids measured within the Krebs cycle will give vital clues of deficiencies of nutrients. Metabolic blocks within the Krebs cycle can give rise to inflammation and obesity.

Fats in the diet, as an example, are broken down into fatty acids and churned through the Krebs cycle to produce energy. In the absence of specific nutrients and an amino acid called carnitine, the fatty acids get stored in lipid peroxisomes which are stored as fat or adipose tissue. Carnitine acts as a taxi delivering fatty acids to the mitochondria for energy production. A diet low in carnitine is typical in vegetarians and during periods of significant stress.

The primary metabolic blocks that may contribute towards fat deposition are:

* **appetite regulatory network dysfunction**
* **insulin sensitivity or resistance**
* **adrenal stress dysfunction**
* **diet**
* **exercise**
* **lifestyle**
* **hormonal imbalance**
* **thyroid imbalance**
* **imbalances in neurotransmitters**
* **genetics**
* **inflammation**

Optimising just one of these factors probably won't result in long-term weight loss. It's important to address all contributing factors to obesity simultaneously.

Why Would Sita Gain Weight?

Sita is by no means obese but is uncomfortable with weight around her hips and thighs, back, under the arms and under the boobs. Her weight gain is regulated by very important neuropeptides that will let her brain know if she has an appetite or feeling full. The key to controlling Sita's weight gain is to balance the hormones in the brain that regulate appetite.

Just when you thought neurotransmitters are the be all and end all of the brain chemicals... *wait*, there's more! They're called neuropeptides and they affect appetite. An imbalance of these neuropeptides can stimulate or inhibit the appetite. Various weight loss programs use specific nutrients or drugs that may play a role in stimulating or inhibiting these brain neuropeptides.

The regulation of appetite involves highly complex systems in the brain. The appetite hormones, or neuropeptides, play critical roles in the control of food intake and obesity. Let's examine neurotransmitters and neuropeptides in weight gain!

What Do Neurotransmitters have to do with Appetite?

The key to controlling the appetite regulatory network in the brain is to balance neurotransmitters like serotonin, dopamine and GABA, decrease inflammation markers like C-reactive protein and interleukin-6 and improve insulin resistance.

In obesity, there is a tendency to:
* **lack motivation (could be due to low serotonin or low dopamine)**
* **gain weight irrespective of dieting (could be due to low thyroid high cortisol or insulin resistance)**
* **crave sugars (could be due to low serotonin, low dopamine or insulin resistance)**
* **feel exhausted (could be due to low thyroid, low adrenals, low dopamine, low glutamate, or low adrenaline)**
* **feel anxious (could be due to low serotonin and low GABA, high adrenaline, high glutamate or high cortisol)**
* **feel low, flat or depressed (could be due to low serotonin, low thyroid, low vitamin D or high glutamate)**

Low serotonin levels can contribute to carbohydrate cravings leading to elevated sugar, which in turn further lowers serotonin. This is why we crave sugars and refined carbohydrates. Carbohydrates increase serotonin. Protein tends to lack this effect on serotonin.[46]

Symptoms of cravings, lack of motivation, anxiety, and depression, which leads to sleep disturbances and poor resistance to pain are prevalent with low serotonin.

Diets low in tryptophan lead to low serotonin. The brain senses that you're starving so it stimulates the appetite. Low serotonin levels result in the preference for carbohydrates. Serotonin levels decrease when you diet.

Dopamine on the other hand, is a reward and motivation hormone. Appetite is controlled by the brain's limbic region through dopamine release. In obesity, dopamine signalling and its receptors are reduced. This is why a depletion in dopamine leads to addiction.[47]

GABA, the natural calmer, improves glucose tolerance and insulin sensitivity. GABA has been shown to reduce adipocyte or fat cell mass and increase intestinal fluid secretion thereby regulating the gut function.

Stress and Weight

When the body is under stress, cortisol is released, which talks to the brain to react to the stress. The brain releases adrenaline to react to stress, in what is called the 'adrenalin rush'. This adrenaline rush acts to mop up glucose from the blood as food for energy. The brain gets its energy from the release of noradrenaline, adrenaline and glucagon.

Once the glucose stores in the blood have been used up to react to stress, the brain signals to the pancreas to release insulin. Insulin needs glucose to function. The quickest form of food or glucose is achieved from the breakdown of muscle tissue. This process is called gluconeogenesis, and it occurs in the liver. Adrenaline then signals the liver to stimulate a process called gluconeogenesis and glycogenolysis.

It is not unusual to eat more when stressed. Stress changes the gears in the car – the adrenal glands go into full throttle. Stress promotes storage of food in fat cells. Addiction to the 'high' feeling is common when the body is in an 'adrenaline rush' state. When the adrenal glands have been stressed for a prolonged period of time, one needs to fill the tank up with coffee, soft drinks, and sugar, more often.

The desperate need for a sugar fix initiates a tendency to binge eat. The increase in blood sugar may contribute toward symptoms of a foggy brain, shakiness, nausea and trembling.

Why Not Use Fat for Energy?

Glycogenolysis is a process of breaking down fat for energy. In other words, it's too hard to break down fat for immediate energy. Instead, muscle tissue breaks down to release amino acids, which convert to energy. As the muscles break down, they become sore, shaky and tired. This is why Sita feels tired and has muscle aches and pains that eventually leads to ketoacidosis and lactic acidosis.

The Sugar Fix

The body releases glucagon, adrenaline, and cortisol as a natural response to low blood sugar.

Increased blood sugar will sensitise insulin, eventually leading to insulin resistance. Insulin resistance is a common cause of weight gain since the body is not processing glucose. High levels of insulin will increase fat deposition and decreases fat burning for energy. This becomes a predicament for inflammatory conditions like cardiovascular disease, hormonal depletion and immune dysregulation. The same level of dysregulation can be seen in people with low cortisol or those who have a poor diet.

Stress, therefore releases cortisol and adrenaline, increases blood sugar, causes glycaemic dysregulation and leads to central obesity – the belly fat pad!

Adrenaline signals the pancreas to release glucagon and insulin. Insulin needs glucose to function. Yeah! Let's have sugar!

When the insulin and glucagon systems are out of balance insulin resistance results. Let's picture the insulin receptor as a lock and the brain behind the door. The brain needs glucose and has sent signals off to the pancreas to release insulin. Insulin needs to turn the lock in order for the glucose to enter the brain. If the lock is jammed, the brain becomes starved. On the other side of the door appetite has already been stimulated for that urgent need of a sugar fix, but the sugar is on the other side of the brain. When insulin finally unlocks onto the correct receptor, the lock is unjammed and the brain receives a rush of glucose. This defect of insulin on its receptors eventually leads to a condition called insulin resistance (IR). Insulin resistance is the trigger to all the inflammatory conditions like metabolic syndrome, cardiovascular disease, high blood pressure, high cholesterol, and diabetes. Correcting insulin and blood glucose levels is paramount to inflammation of any kind in the body.

When to Eat, How Much to Eat, When to Stop?

Healthy weight is a result of balance between appetite stimulation and satiety or the feeling of fullness. Important brain chemicals, which we call appetite regulatory complex, control appetite and satiety. When the balance is lost, obesity and weight gain can result. The balance is regulated by brain chemicals, primarily insulin, leptin, ghrelin, cholestakynin, cortisol, and adiponectin.[48]

The brain is responsible for appetite and satiety. A symphony of neuropeptides and hormones in the brain regulate the appetite, namely, leptin and adiponectin.

Some of the notable appetite hormones include the following:

* **amylin – a polypeptide that decreases the appetite through slowing gastric emptying**
* **PP, pancreatic polypeptide reduces appetite by signalling fullness**
* **GLP-1, glucagon like peptide enhances insulin secretion and suppresses glucagon secretion after a meal to suppress appetite**
* **OXM, – oxyntomodulin, an amino acid peptide that suppresses ghrelin from intestinal cells**
* **NPY, neuropeptide Y that stimulates feeling of hunger**

Why Is Sita Struggling to Lose Weight?

Her weight gain could be a result of an imbalanced signal of the neuropeptides in the appetite regulatory complex.

The brain chemicals responsible for appetite stimulation and suppression are governed by the appetite regulatory complex. Hormones like leptin and adiponectin regulate satiety or feeling full through brain pathways that regulate food intake.

The pancreas, stomach, and intestine are stimulated by the hypothalamus, brainstem, and vagal efference in the brain, which in turn works with the appetite regulatory complex.

The key appetite regulatory network hormones that decrease appetite are CCK (cholestakynin), a gut peptide; leptin, an adipose hormone; and insulin, a pancreatic hormone.

The neuropeptides that increase appetite are cortisol, an adrenal hormone and ghrelin, a gut hormone.[49]

Craving Sweet Things Late at Night

Low blood sugar triggers hunger for carbohydrates. Insulin regulates glucose release into the bloodstream. In obesity insulin sensitivity decreases, leading to increased levels of insulin needed for blood sugar balancing or homeostasis (a state of balance).

Macronutrients in the diet release gut peptides to support and influence intestinal motility and provide feedback to the hypothalamus which is in charge of regulating the appetite regulatory complex. CCK is a gut peptide that together with insulin and leptin reduces appetite or provide a feeling of satiety.[50]

In *leptin* resistance, *leptin* level is *high*, which means you might be overweight, but your brain can't see it. In other words, the brain is starved, while the body is obese. That's what obesity is: it's starving the brain! Leptin sends signals from the brain when fat stores are adequate. Leptin is an adipocyte hormone that regulates the size of fat stores. Obese people have an unusually high circulating concentration of leptin, suggesting that obesity is associated with insensitivity to leptin or leptin resistance. Obese people generally produce higher levels of leptin, but they become resistant or unresponsive to its signals. Instead they operate in a false state of leptin deficiency, which leads to increased serotonin release and stimulated appetite.[51]

Leptin and serotonin work hand-in-hand. When the leptin-serotonin pathway is turned on, appetite increases, and when the pathway is turned off, appetite decreases.

Adiponectin production slows down in obesity, in states of insulin resistance and diabetes. Adiponectin lowers glucose and improves insulin sensitivity to promote weight loss.

Stress induces both ghrelin and cortisol. Ghrelin stimulates appetite by lowering leptin levels causing patients to become more efficient at storing fat and getting fatter.

Ghrelin is a gut peptide that stimulates appetite by lowering leptin levels. Imbalance in ghrelin and leptin can prevent lipolysis , the breakdown of fat or lipogenesis, the build-up of fat stores in the body. Ghrelin also increases hunger.

Does Sleep Affect Weight?

A lack of sleep elevates inflammation and cortisol levels leading to weight gain. Beyond balancing homeostatic needs, sleep, and neuromodulation are at the core of how the nervous system is able to form and consolidate new memories.

Lack of sleep is linked to increased ghrelin or appetite, decreased leptin or satiety and therefore difficulty in losing weight.

Less than 5 hours of sleep is equivalent to 15% more calories consumed than with regular 6 to 8 hours of sleep.[52]

What Happens to Hormones in Obesity?

Balancing brain neurotransmitters helps obesity in that it increases:
* **serotonin which decreases carbohydrate cravings**
* **serotonin which counters excess cortisol**
* **dopamine which reduces addictions**

Balancing neurotransmitters therefore sets the stage for balanced appetite signalling!

Improving the Balance Between Appetite and Satiety

To improve the balance between appetite and satiety, firstly, we need to stimulate and improve the levels of neuropeptides like leptin and ghrelin. Secondly, balance neurotransmitters like serotonin and dopamine and stress hormone, cortisol. Thirdly, regulate insulin, glucose intolerance and inflammation.

Weight gain is a multifactorial problem. It can be associated with:
* **food allergies**
* **hormonal dysregulation**
* **thyroid dysfunction**
* **appetite regulatory complex neuropeptide imbalances**
* **neurotransmitter imbalances**

* **sleep deprivation**
* **toxic exposure**
* **inflammation**
* **nutrient depletion**
* **lack of exercise**

Allergies and Weight

Allergy sufferers might unknowingly crave foods that they're sensitive, intolerant or allergic to. Allergenic foods can set off chemical reactions and neurotransmitter imbalances. People get addicted to get a 'high' feeling from eating foods that start an inflammatory allergenic response. Allergies elicit immune responses. When the immune complexes are formed, the body retains fluid in its attempt to dilute the complexes. Excess fluid contributes towards weight gain.

The foods causing the most allergies are gluten, dairy, eggs and nuts. Food allergies influence the limbic region of the brain, which is associated with feeling hungry. The greater the intolerance to a food, the greater the craving for that food.

Hormones and Weight

Hormone levels go out of balance with age. As progesterone declines in menopause, for example, estrogens become dominant. Estrogens, being a proliferative hormone, has the capacity to increase insulin sensitivity. It is quite common to see weight gain in states of hormonal imbalance as in perimenopause, menopause and andropause.

A woman with polycystic ovarian syndrome (PCOS) will invariably be insulin resistant. Regulating glucose levels is essential in PCOS.

Testosterone declines in the ageing male. Low levels of testosterone affects insulin release, which might develop as a pot belly.

Low thyroid function slows down metabolism of fats, carbohydrates, and protein leading to weight gain.

Weight gain sets up *inflammation* which leads to chronic diseases. Fat cells make adipokines that stimulate chronic inflammation. Leptin inhibits food intake and activates thermogenesis together with insulin. Leptin helps tame the appetite and boosts metabolism.

In a *candida* infection, the yeast feeds on sugar. Candida growth can lead to leaky gut and weight gain.

How to Manage the Battle of the Bulge

Losing weight depends on appetite and the number of calories and the types of foods consumed. Stress encourages consumption of comfort food. An overactive appetite is associated with an imbalance or disordered level of the brain chemicals that regulate appetite. The symphony of neuropeptide signals regulate appetite. Suppressing the brain chemicals that regulate appetite is the key to weight loss.

> *'To lengthen thy life, lessen thy meals.'* Benjamin Franklin

Studies have shown that 20 to 25% decrease in caloric intake may extend life by 10 to 20%.[53]

Exercise for a Fit Brain

What if we had a 'drug' that could help to alleviate obesity, depression, decrease aggressive behaviour, increase cognitive function, help with attention span, improve sleep quality and potentially influence the gut microbiome at a relatively inexpensive cost.

We have that 'drug'! It's called exercise!

Behaviour is a product of how we think and feel. Being overweight increases the risk of major diseases. The direct and indirect costs of obesity puts a significant financial load on the public purse. Get moving!

Exercise is essential for increasing metabolic rate, burning fat and sensitising insulin.

It is advisable to do a minimum of 3 hours of exercise per week. Incorporate three types of exercise for optimal results such as:

* **circulation exercise (to get the blood flowing like dancing, running, walking, tennis, swimming)**

* resistance exercise (to build muscle mass and burn fat like weights, resistance classes, or pump classes)
* grounding and strengthening exercises (to manage the mind and maintain flexibility like yoga, meditation, Pilates, tai chi)

Sita's Natural Weight Management Strategies

Assessment of Sita's neurotransmitters, stress hormones and appetite regulatory hormones revealed a depletion of serotonin, elevated levels of cortisol, blood glucose, oestrogens and leptin.

How do these chemistries affect Sita's weight?
* **High cortisol gives rise to high stress, muscle aches and pains and weight gain.**
* **Low Serotonin gives rise to insulin resistance and the need for a sugar fix.**
* **High blood glucose may be a precursor for diabetes.**
* **High leptin or leptin resistance struggle to shut down appetite.**
* **Elevated oestrogens are responsible for visceral adiposity**

Sita initiated a structured and regular exercise regime together with a wholesome, fresh organic diet. Sita's battle of the bulge required supplementation aimed specifically to supress appetite, maintain the feeling of fullness, stimulate metabolism and prevent fat adiposity.

The key to weight loss is a reduction of body weight, abdominal fat mass, managing carbohydrate cravings, slowing the absorption of dietary fat from the intestine, and supporting leptin sensitivity. Shedding weight can add years to your life. Studies have shown that if Australians lost as little as 5 kg, it could result in 34% reduction in deaths associated with cardiovascular disease.[54]

The weight loss industry is a constant money spinner! Numerous weight loss regimes are available on the marketplace each claiming to be better than the other. One diet does not suit all. It is important to structure diet to suit the individual taking into account underlying causative factors and correcting them.

Sita supplemented her diet with a compound formula containing garcinia, irvingia, and l-carnitine. In addition, stress was managed with adrenal herbs and estrogen dominance with indole-3-carbinols. She was advised to incorporate foods to remediate glucose intolerance and assist her with the 'sugar fix' including bitter melon, fenugreek and cinnamon tea.

She reported a significant shift in weight once stress was managed and hormones were balanced. The addition of supplements to stimulate metabolism, prevent fat from being absorbed and use fat for energy was the 'cherry on the cake' in attaining the ideal body weight. Numerous nutrients and supplements are available for weight management.

Principles of notable supplements for weight management:

* **l-carnitine is an amino acid made from lysine and methionine necessary for fat metabolism and utilisation.**
* **Conjugated linoleic acid is a good oil that improves insulin sensitivity and promotes weight loss.**
* **Green tea decreases body weight and waist circumference by stimulating thermogenesis. Studies have shown that green tea decreased mean body weight by 4.61% and mean waist circumference by 4.48%.**[55]
* **Cocoa supports healthy eating patterns and manages carbohydrate cravings. Components of cocoa regulate certain neurotransmitters involved in appetite, hunger and mood regulation.**
* **Pepper and piper longum support weight loss by uncoupling proteins involved in energy expenditure and thermoregulation.**
* **Garcinia from mangosteen fruit allows fat storing cells called adipocytes to become metabolically dysfunctional and bloated. Garcinia elevates levels of adiponectin which sends signals to fat cells to break down for energy utilisation.**
* **Irvingia from African mango inhibits the enzyme involved in the conversion of glucose and triglycerides into fat cells. Irvingia can inhibit enzyme alpha amylase which supports a slower rate of carbohydrate absorption and reduces the caloric impact of starchy and sugary foods.**[56]

Could You Be Obese? Take the Quiz!

◊ *What is your body mass index?*
 * obese, greater than 30 kg/m^2
 * overweight, between 25–29 kg/m^2
 * underweight, less than 18.5 kg/m^2
◊ *How many hours per week do you engage in physical activity?*
◊ *Does obesity run in your family?*

- *How many hours of the day is spent being sedentary or inactive?*
- *Do you follow healthy dietary guidelines?*
- *Do you have an MTHFR gene mutation?*

Calculate the number of answers you've circled against the total number of possible results. If you scored more than 30% of the checklist, you may have an imbalance. It is important to investigate your body chemistry with validated functional laboratory testing. (See Chapter 15)

11

The Toxic Brain

The 'toxic brain' may play a significant role in mental health. Mental health disorders have increased with the enormous amounts of toxic metals in the environment and the widespread nutrient mineral insufficiencies of the modern diet.

The inability of the liver to detoxify effectively can be a major contributing factor to mental health conditions like stress, anxiety, depression, ADD or Alzheimer's. Toxins in the environment, in foods, and in the air may have an impact on genetic mutations which affect mood.

Harry's Story

Harry, a 45-year-old third-generation farmer, has been suffering severe depression in line with a series of traumas within a short space of time. His traumas consisted of the loss of his wife, financial strain and drought. He was unable to cope with the stresses and the adjustments following the grief of losing his wife. He complained of being forgetful and overwhelmed.

He had been an active, hard-working farmer all his life. He said, 'I'm a different person now. Life is not worth living.' He had been prescribed an SSRI for his depression. Although he felt much better since initiating his antidepressant medication, he was determined to investigate the underlying causes of the sudden change within him.

Harry had been using various pesticides and herbicides on his farm. Being a third generation farmer, he had been exposed to chemicals like pesticides from birth.

Where Does Toxicity Come From?

Toxic exposure is a growing concern worldwide. There are thousands of chemicals registered for use within the cosmetic, agricultural, and veterinary and food industries. Every year, thousands of new chemicals are approved by the Environmental Protection Agency (EPA) for use in humans or in agriculture. The safety levels of toxins vary in each country due to respective EPA regulations.

Pervasive chemical compounds disrupt the immune, nervous and endocrine systems. As more toxic chemicals are used in every facet of our daily lives, there continues to be an increase in infertility, allergies, chemical sensitivities, hormonal imbalances and cancer. One major culprit is glyphosate, a well-known commonly used pesticide, also known as Roundup, which has been shown to cause and worsen modern diseases.

Some compounds may become toxic when mixed with other chemicals, and in fact some toxic chemicals may actually enhance the toxic capability of others.

Harry's Toxicities

Harry is a third generation farmer. He has been exposed to pesticides while in utero and throughout his life.

He had a hair tissue mineral and metal analysis performed that revealed high levels of mercury, lead and arsenic. Glyphosates in his blood were reported as being high. His mineral levels were marginally deficient. He wanted to investigate treating heavy metal toxicity naturally.

He has had a physically active working life. This implies that his robust metabolism in the country air with a wholesome diet was sufficient to naturally deal with toxic exposures. As he aged, and the stresses mounted, the body failed to respond the same way. Instead, toxins that have accumulated, now lodge in parts of the brain and other organ systems resulting in chronic health conditions. When heavy metals and environmental pollutants lodge in the brain cells, they have the potential to develop amyloid plaques, or hardening of the neural pathways, leading to complex degenerative mental health conditions like senile dementia and Alzheimer's. Hardening of the arteries is associated with cardiovascular disease. Hardening of the neural pathways in the brain is a serious mental health concern.

Stress and subsequent adrenal insufficiency can cause brain fog and an inability to cope. Harry is stressed and depressed. His prescription SSRI medication is helping him cope with grief and depressive episodes.

Harry's mineral and metal results indicated toxic levels of mercury, lead and arsenic. In the city, exposure to chemical and environmental pollutants is predominantly in the air and through diet in the form of pesticides and herbicides

Harry's glyphosate levels were high. Glyphosate (aka Roundup), a powerful weed killer, which, when accumulated over years of exposure through occupation, diet or water supplies, can contribute towards serious health risks. Glyphosate mixed up with solvents, work together to amplify the toxic effects of the herbicide.

Glyphosates have been shown to:
* **boost antibiotic resistance**
* **cause disruption in the microbial function of the gut**
* **deplete nutrient composition of crops**
* **inhibit detoxification processes**
* **be associated with infertility, cancer and behavioural changes**

Drug associated toxicity affects the liver. People who are on lots of medication long-term put a huge strain on the liver. Medication, together with a poor diet, alcohol, smoking or recreational drugs tend to compound toxicity, further compromising detoxification processes of the liver.[57]

Can Drugs Cause Depression?

Some pharmaceutical medications have side effects of sadness and depression. Drugs that might cause mood changes varying from mania to elation may include:

- corticosteroids
- cyclosporine
- levo dopa
- antidepressants
- amphetamine
- antimalarial drugs
- anticonvulsants
- barbiturates
- benzodiazepines
- beta-blockers
- calcium channel blockers
- opiates painkillers
- statins
- antivirals

Stimulants such as alcohol or recreational drugs are other major contributing factors for mental health conditions. Continued use of pharmaceutical medication alongside toxic exposure puts a significant load on the liver to perform detoxification processes.

Heavy metals and environmental pollutants are found in the food chain, and particularly also in megacities. Heavy metal toxicity is not a new phenomenon.

Mad As a Hatter and Toxic Exposure

In the 18th century, workers in England who made felt hats were exposed to mercury. This element is highly toxic to the brain. The hatters became mad due to exposure of mercury and the absorption of toxins such as solvents, chemicals, and other heavy metals in the process of making hats.

Heavy metal toxicity can also lead to numerous health conditions including those affecting the various body systems – cardiovascular, endocrine, immune, musculo-skeletal, and integumentary and nervous systems. Mechanisms of toxicity include antagonism of mineral balance, alterations in enzyme activity, and changes in neuronal membrane potential, increased oxidation and the effects on the immune system.

The signs and symptoms that a person may experience depend upon the type of metal, its form, the quantity, the length of exposure, the type of exposure, the age of the person, and the person's general state of health.

A serious metal overload can damage the blood–brain barrier, promoting damaging effects of toxins in the brain, called "leaky brain". Key nutrients typically used in the brain may deplete reducing the concentration of neurotransmitter concentration and neurotransmission along myelin sheaths.

Today, we have a much bigger problem. A highly industrialised culture gives scope for environmental toxic exposure, be it in the form of industrial waste or in the perfume you wear. Heavy metals and chemicals are found in carpet, in a new car, or in the very air you breathe. Most can tolerate exposure to chemicals because the immune system and liver are capable of fighting the toxic effects and detoxifying the chemicals. If the immune system is weak, the body cannot fight chemical exposure. The chemicals become toxic to the body, which over time, brings on symptoms of mood swings, irritability, depression, memory loss, seizures and tics.

Smog in Our Brains

The yellow grey haze of smog hovering over the skyline can have deleterious effects on the body and create havoc on the mind. Researchers have found that high levels of air pollution can harm cardiovascular and respiratory health, increasing the risk of mental health disorders and giving a lower life expectancy. The EPA (Environmental Protection Agency) has established standards for pollution. Long-term exposure to air pollution can damage the brain and lead to learning difficulties, memory problems and depression. The brain becomes inflamed when breathing polluted air.

Heavy Metals

Heavy metals play an integral role in industrialised culture. Metals like aluminium, cadmium, lead and mercury are found in air and food, in industrial, household and personal products.

These metals are rapidly removed from blood circulation and shunted away to tissue storage sites in vital tissues such as the heart, brain, kidneys, bone, or liver where they disrupt our biological systems. They displace vital nutritional minerals from where they should be in the body to provide biological function. For example, instead of calcium being present in an enzyme reaction, lead or cadmium take its place. Toxic metals can't fulfil the same role as the nutritional minerals, thus their presence becomes critically disruptive to enzyme activity.

Although they can be found in high concentrations in the body, a number of these heavy metals (aluminium, beryllium, cadmium, lead and mercury) have no known biological function. Others (arsenic, copper, iron and nickel) are thought to be essential at low concentrations, but are toxic at high levels.

Heavy metals are either inhaled, ingested or absorbed by the skin. Toxicity occurs when the metals displace the essential elements in the body and begin to affect the normal function of various organs. Acute or chronic exposures occur in the workplace, especially in industries that use metals to manufacture products, such as the cadmium, lead, and mercury used in batteries and the arsenic used in some pesticides. Exposure can also occur in agricultural workers, in people whose job it is to clean up contaminated environmental sites, in those who work with certain products, such as auto mechanics working with car batteries, and in those with hobbies that involve the use of metals – such as the lead used by stained glass artisans.

Elevated levels of iron, copper and zinc are related to neurodegenerative diseases such as Alzheimer's disease and Parkinson's disease.[58]

The unifying factor in the manifestations of heavy metal exposure (particularly of arsenic, lead, cadmium and mercury) is oxidative stress.

Fish and Mercury: the dilemma of potential mercury toxicity in fish is a growing concern. Fortunately, organic and inorganic mercury can be measured to differentiate the safety of eating fish or the toxic effects of dental mercury amalgams. The relationship between mercury and selenium is important. Selenium found in tuna fish, as an example has the capacity to antagonise mercury known to be present in fish, which renders the tuna safe.

Lead: Lead may be found in leaded paint, leaded gasoline, painted dishes, toys from China, candy from Mexico, some jewellery, and sometimes canned foods.

Cadmium toxicity develops from both smoking and passive exposure to smoking.

Aluminium toxicity may develop with continued cooking in aluminium pots or antiperspirants.

Heavy Metals and Behaviour

Heavy metal toxicity can have a wide range of negative effects, such as the following.

- **Mercury can cause depression, allergies and anxiety; mercury and cadmium can significantly compromise your immune system. Amalgam fillings are slowly being phased out in dental work but still present a significant risk of mercury poisoning.**
- **Lead poisoning disturbs GABA balance, which contributes to anxiety, worry and insomnia.**
- **Lead, cadmium, and arsenic toxicity can inhibit dopamine synthesis causing low mood and motivation.**
- **Mercury, lead and aluminium disturb acetylcholine responsible for memory, concentration and focus**

Mercury toxicity is prevalent in those with low vitamin B5. Mercury binds to sulphur compounds such as methionine, cysteine, lipoic acid, and thiamine, compromising the availability of the essential nutrients to the body.

Aluminium competes with *magnesium* binding sites, so low magnesium can accelerate accumulation of aluminium in the brain and zinc deficiency can augment this accumulation.

Lead induces neurotoxicity blocking glutaminergic synaptic activity which in turn can alter synaptic plasticity manifesting as memory decline.

Food Additives as Toxins

Food additives, dyes and flavours are used extensively in the diet to enhance the appearance, and flavour of food and prolong shelf life.

People with mental health disorders and chronic diseases will benefit from eating fresh, wholesome foods free from additives, preservatives, and flavour enhancing ingredients as found in processed food.

Food dyes and preservatives found in a variety of common foods like soft drinks, fruit juices, cereals, and processed food can cause mood disorders, particularly hyperactivity in children. Low blood sugar or hypoglycaemia causes the brain to secrete glutamate in higher levels, which can lead to agitation, depression, anger, panic attacks and anxiety.

Monosodium glutamate (MSG) is a popular flavour enhancer in Chinese or canned foods and raises glutamate to toxic levels. Glutamate is an excitatory neurotransmitter. When in excess, it becomes an excitotoxin acting like a poison to the brain. Adverse effects of MSG may present as aggression, agitation, irrational behaviour, depression, fatigue, headaches and weight gain.

Artificial sweeteners also act as neurotoxins and carcinogens. They are found in baked goods, toothpaste, cereals and soft drinks.

High fructose corn syrup is a highly refined artificial sweetener found in many processed foods, predominantly in America and western societies, which includes bread, flavoured yoghurts, canned vegetables and cereals.

Trans-fats are used to enhance and extend the shelf life of food and are found in fried fast foods or partly cooked frozen foods, margarine, chips, crackers and baked goods.

Common food dyes like tartrazine or a red dye, have been associated with chromosomal damage and impaired brain nerve function. They're found in lollies or sweets, cereal, soft drinks, sports drinks, pet food and ice cream.

Sodium sulphide, a preservative used in winemaking and dried fruit, can cause asthmatic attacks headaches, breathing problems and rashes.

Sodium nitrite, which is used as a preservative and as a colour and flavour in bacon, ham, sausages, hotdogs or deli meats has been associated with liver and pancreatic problems.

BHA and BHT (butylated hydroxy toluene) preservatives are found in cereals, potato chips and vegetable oils. This preservative keeps foods from changing colour, changing flavour or becoming rancid.

Sulphur dioxide, found in beer, soft drinks, dried fruit, juices, wine and potato products, has been associated with reactions such as bronchial problems, hypotension, flushing and tingling sensations.

Environmental Pollutants

Increasing exposure to environmental pollutants has been linked to many chronic diseases and mental health disorders.

Various toxic chemicals have been found to disrupt the immune and nervous systems and the brain, leading to a number of chronic conditions. Some of these toxicants can play a role in mental health disorders and chronic diseases include the following.

* **Alkylphenols** – found in everyday products. These toxicants are used as surfactants in detergents. Examples of alkylphenols are bisphenol A, triclosan used in plastics, water bottles, baby bottles, deodorants, toothpaste and cleaning supplies.
* **DDT (dichlorodiphenyltrichloroethane)** is an organochlorine insecticide used in agriculture and is commonly found in meat, poultry and fish. These compounds persist in the environment today despite some countries banning DDT.
* **Organophosphates** are insecticides that are considered to be toxic to animals. They are used on crops as insect control, mosquito repellent and on livestock.
* **Plasticisers** such as phthalates and parabens are usually added as stabilisers in cosmetics, shampoos, medical bags and as food additives.
* **Polychlorinated biphenyls (PCBs)** have been introduced in the 1970s as industrial chemicals. PCBs are often found in contaminated food, Atlantic salmon, farmed fish, inks, flame retardants, plasticizers and contaminated water.
* **Volatile solvents** such as styrene, xylene and benzenes are found in common household products including cleaning and polishing fluids, spray-on personal care items, nail polish remover, paint and glues.

Assessing Toxicity

Symptoms of heavy metals poisoning are identical to symptoms of neurological and psychiatric disorders. Therefore, it is difficult or impossible to identify their cause without laboratory testing.

It is equally important to measure levels of minerals that play an essential part in numerous physiochemical reactions such as transformation of energy or elimination of toxins in the body.

Heavy metal testing can be performed on a hair, urine or blood sample. Analysis of mineral and metal levels in a hair sample is a measure of:

* **minerals – such as sodium, potassium, calcium or magnesium**
* **trace elements – such as lithium, vanadium, rubidium**
* **toxic metals – including arsenic, cadmium, mercury and lead.**

Hair testing represents long-standing exposure as hair traps and stores all these elements between strands of keratin, the protein that comprises around 95% of hair tissue.

Blood and urine can reflect exposures that are chronic or that have happened in the previous few days. Blood provides information about what the body has currently or recently absorbed. Blood levels are largely independent of tissue deposition. Blood analysis measures both extracellular and intracellular levels.

Urine is an appropriate sample to assess the excretion of potentially toxic elements, providing a window on levels retained in the body and indicating duration of exposure, especially significant diagnostically because of the prevailing patterns of exposure. Urine testing is reflective of metabolic exposure, and therefore provides good qualitative information of recent toxic exposure.

Exposure to environmental pollutants can be measured in urine or blood samples.

Treatment Strategies

Treatment of any metal or chemical exposure may include removing the source of exposure once identified and clearing the effects of those toxins in the body through specific detoxification procedures.

If the toxicant happens to be a food additive, remove the food, and find a suitable alternative. If mercury toxicity has been identified perhaps as a result of mercury-based dental fillings, arrange for the dentist to remove them and replace with safer alternatives.

Detoxification should be performed to eliminate the risk of recirculation of the toxicants once dislodged. In some cases, though, detoxification can be damaging to organ tissue and therefore needs to be performed with medical guidance. The purpose of detoxification is to protect against toxicant damage from inflammation, oxidative stress, mitochondrial injury and mental health disturbance.

Detoxification can take place by:
* **use of pharmaceutical chelators or sequestering agents such as deferoxamine**
* **liver, gall bladder and kidney herbal detoxification**

Intravenous chelation requires infusion of nutrients through the blood. Detoxifying heavy metals involves balancing mineral antagonists that dislodge the metals from the tissues into the blood with chelating agents that bind the metals and prevent them from being re-deposited somewhere else, so then the kidneys excretes them. Regular detoxification techniques like fasting, liver flush, and kidney cleansers have limited effect with heavy metals.

It's essential that all phases of detoxification are functioning well and are in balance to avoid accumulation of potentially harmful intermediates.

Adequate nutrition is vital for efficient detoxification, especially for phase II conjugation reactions, which are heavily dependent on amino acids, and therefore dietary protein.

Treatment Strategies for Harry

Harry's hair tissue mineral and metal analysis revealed toxic levels of mercury, lead and arsenic. His glyphosate levels were high. It was established that toxic exposure through occupation had contributed to high levels of metals and glyphosate. Recent bouts of stress with age compromised the immune system's ability to cope with the toxicants he could tolerate adequately in the past.

Management of stress with appropriate psychotherapy, antidepressant medication and adrenal herbal intervention is essential. He had reported that he was feeling better being on the antidepressants and felt less stressed with adrenal herbs. Harry initiated a natural and targeted heavy metal detoxification program aimed to treat the liver and gallbladder. During the treatment, he was instructed to increase the intake of water to two litres per day, incorporate regular exercise and enjoy an infrared sauna three times a week. Exercise assists in circulation and hepatic detoxification. The herbal detox program proved effective for him, and hence the option of IV chelation was ruled out.

Metal toxicant levels were re-examined 3 months later. Harry felt much healthier, lighter and cleaner on the inside. He felt at ease and stable emotionally, and was ready to discuss reduction of antidepressant dose with his doctor.

Agents used in detoxification include the following.

* **Amino acids such as taurine, glycine, glutamine, N-acetyl cysteine (NAC). Cysteine is a very efficient and cost-effective chelating agent. It chelates mercury, lead, cadmium and arsenic. Cysteine is a sulphur containing amino acid. Flooding the body with extra sulphur at the same time satisfies the body's other competing needs for sulphur and preserves cysteine.**
* **N-acetyl cysteine is an activated form of cysteine which increases glutathione to promote liver detoxification and enhances the elimination of heavy metals.[59]**
* **Supplementation with antioxidants alongside chelation therapy has proven to be a better treatment regime than chelation therapy alone (such as alpha lipoic acid, green tea).**
* **Certain antioxidants including vitamin C and E, alpha lipoic acid, glutathione are especially beneficial in heavy metal toxicity.[60]**
* **Selenium can dislodge mercury stored in the brain which may enter circulation to be stored in the liver or kidney and with appropriate detoxification be excreted effectively.**
* **Herbs such as milk thistle, bupleurum, cape jasmine, coriander, and parsley.**
* **Polyphenols such as found in chlorophyll and green tea.**
* **Probiotics such as arabinogalactans.**
* **Sulphur rich diet e.g. garlic, onions, and eggs. Clinoptilolite is a naturally occurring volcanic mineral with a unique crystalline structure, a type of zeolite. Clinoptilolite assists in safely binding and removing heavy metals from the body.[61]**
* **Chelating agents such as EDTA (ethylenediamine tetraacetic acid), DMPS (2,3-dimercaptopropane-1-sulphonic acid) and DMSA (dimercaptosuccinic acid) are considered to be the best known treatment for metal poisoning but may have serious side effects.**

Prescriptive measures involve injections or oral therapy of DMSA, DMPS and EDTA together with powerful antioxidant support.

Intravenous chelation therapy uses specific chelating agents like vitamin C, glutathione, lipoic acid to bind toxins and heavy metals in the blood and allowing them to be flushed out of the body in urine, sweat and stool. The IV method bypasses digestive system, allowing targeted elimination of toxicants without unwanted side effects.

Do You Have a Heavy Metal Toxicity? Take the Quiz!

- *Do you smoke?*
- *Have you been exposed to passive smoking?*
- *Do you drink tap water?*
- *Do you have copper or galvanised iron water pipes?*
- *Do you have amalgam fillings?*
- *Do you use inorganic personal care products (e.g. make-up, deodorant)?*
- *Do you have metal objects in your body (e.g. knee prosthesis, tooth implant)?*
- *Do you use fluoride toothpaste?*
- *Do you live close to a freeway or main road?*
- *Do you live near a mining town or work in the mining industry?*
- *Do you live in a megacity?*
- *Do you live near industrial plants?*
- *Have you renovated or lived in an old house?*
- *Do you use aluminium cooking utensils?*
- *Do you consume canned foods or drinks?*
- *Have you had any CT or MRI scans?*
- *Do you use dye in your hair?*

Calculate the number of answers you've circled against the total number of possible results. If you scored more than 30% of the checklist, you may have an imbalance. It is important to investigate your body chemistry with validated functional laboratory testing. (See Chapter 15)

12

The Copper Head Brain

Neuroscientists have identified specific nutrients that are needed to synthesise and manufacture neurotransmitters, and support gene regulation. Biochemical therapies can adjust the brain levels of these key nutrients.

The primary raw materials for the synthesis of neurotransmitters are nutrients such as amino acids, vitamins and minerals derived from food. The emphasis on pharmaceuticals and statistics on its efficacy has led to interest in published options of both mind-body medicine paradigms as well as targeted nutritional therapy.

Recent scientific advances, particularly in molecular biology of the brain have assisted in providing a road map for the development of effective, natural, drug-free therapies that don't produce serious side effects. This science-based nutrient therapy system can help people diagnosed with mental disorders. Nutrient therapies tailored to specific types of brain chemistries and advances in the latest nutrient-based targeted therapies have been shown to effectively manage mental health disorders like ADHD and schizophrenia.

James's Story

James, a 33-year-old male, was recently diagnosed with schizophrenia. He had been diagnosed with Asperger's syndrome in the past. He had suffered bouts of depression, anger, and manic episodes over many years. Prescription medicines have kept his symptoms at bay to a certain extent. Despite chronic depression, he excelled in college and is successful at his job. He loves singing. He even considered applying for an audition in The Voice. *He was resistant to psychotherapy and chose to use prescription antipsychotics, an SSRI and subsequent SNRI. He was stabilised on prescription medication yet believed that he felt low and flat subsequently.*

He chose to have his nutrient levels examined following research into the value of zinc and copper in mental health. Recent gene tests revealed a genetic mutation of methylation marker.

Nutrients for the Brain

The growing understanding of the impact of nutrients in mental health has birthed the concept of biochemical or nutrient therapy colloquially known as neurobiochemistry. Every person has a unique biochemistry or footprint of genetic factors and biochemical factors that influence mental health, immune system, behaviour and personality. Nutritional needs are unique as 'one man's meat is another man's poison'. In the perfect world, a good diet and lifestyle are all we need for optimum health. However, nutritional needs may not be met by diet alone, hence nutritional supplements are required to overcome genetic aberrations. Balancing zinc and copper is essential for production of neurotransmitters and maintenance of mental health. If copper is in excess in the blood, the prevalence of neurological conditions increases. Other nutrients that play a significant role are vitamin B6, methylating cofactors and essential fatty acids.

Founders of nutrient therapy in mental health, Dr Carl Pfeiffer and Dr Bill Walsh, have studied and published extensively on specific nutrients that may be excessive or deficient in mental health disorders. The common nutrients that cause mental health disturbance are those that make neurotransmitters and those that influence neurotransmitter production or metabolism. These nutrients are copper, iron, folic acid, zinc, molybdenum, manganese, niacin and good oils. Good mental health needs optimal neurotransmitter activity at the synapses.

Assessment of nutrient levels can reveal brain-changing nutrient imbalances in patients diagnosed with attention-deficit/hyperactivity disorder (ADHD), autism, behaviour disorders, depression, schizophrenia and Alzheimer's disease.

The interrelationship of these nutrients correlates closely with methylation and neurotransmitter imbalances. The key to nutrient balance is to normalise the concentration and manufacture of neurotransmitters, regulate gene transcription and reduce oxidative damage.

James' Nutrient Levels

A detailed nutrient assessment of James's lab results revealed:
* **elevated copper, calcium**
* **low zinc, potassium, magnesium, ceruloplasmin**

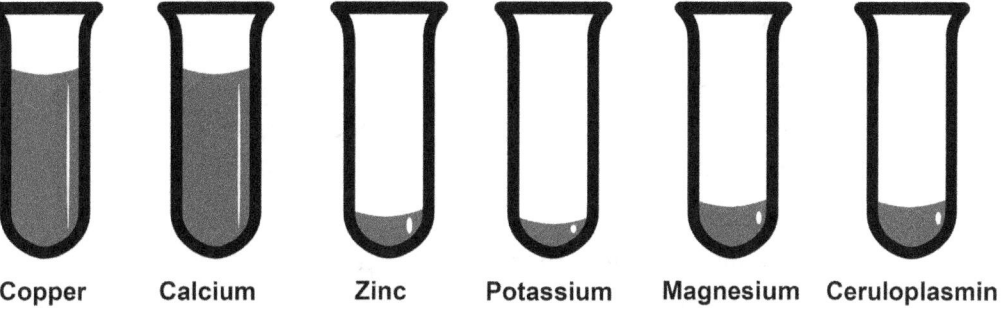

Copper   Calcium   Zinc   Potassium   Magnesium   Ceruloplasmin

Copper

In some mental health conditions like ADD, ADHD and depression, there may be an inability in the sufferer to genetically control copper, zinc, manganese and other elements. The nutrients are transported in the body by a carrier protein called metalothionein. Copper is a necessary cofactor for the synthesis of stress hormones called noradrenaline and adrenaline from dopamine. Copper is needed to regulate immune function, energy metabolism and support cell growth. Too much copper can be damaging to the brain. Elevated copper can cause significant changes in hormone levels.

Copper is transported through the blood attached to a protein or metalothionein called ceruloplasmin. Ceruloplasmin acts as a taxi carting copper from the blood to the tissues where it is required. Copper that is bound to ceruloplasmin is safe and useful in the body. Copper that is not bound to ceruloplasmin is free copper, which is damaging to the body and the brain as it can easily be oxidised. High copper levels can deplete zinc leading to oxidative stress.

Copper in excess is present in most cases of hyperactivity, postpartum depression, autism, and paranoid schizophrenia. Conversely, deficiency of copper is seen in anxiety since copper is needed for dopamine decarboxylase activation. Low copper will therefore slow adrenal hormone production.

When copper is overloaded or in excess, dopamine becomes depleted and noradrenaline increases. High levels of noradrenaline lead to anxiety and conditions like paranoid schizophrenia, bipolar disorder, ADHD and PND.

If you have a copper overload, you're likely to see hyperactivity, skin sensitivity to metals, a metallic taste in the mouth, skin tags, estrogen dominance, emotional meltdown, tinnitus or abnormal periods.

Signs of copper overload:
* **skin sensitivity to metals, flushing, easy bruising**
* **anxiety, depression**
* **headaches**
* **sleep problems**
* **ringing in ears**
* **sensitivity to dyes**
* **hyperactivity**
* **skin tags**
* **irregular menstruation**
* **intolerant behaviour**
* **hypochondria**
* **aggressive, pushy, belligerent**
* **early greying of hair or hair loss.**
* **arthritis**
* **iron deficiency**

If copper is in excess, reduce foods rich in copper, such as:
- almonds
- beans
- crab
- chocolate
- lamb
- mushrooms
- oysters
- pecans
- pork
- prunes
- whole grains

Strategies to reduce copper excess and stimulate metalothionein synthesis and functioning:
- **supplement diet with vitamins C, zinc, molybdenum**
- **supplement with glutamine, histidine and threonine**
- **clearing the copper through liver detoxification and chelation therapy**

Zinc

Zinc is an essential mineral that works in a 'yin-yang' relationship with copper. Zinc is needed for thyroid function, hair, skin, nail production, and cell growth. Low levels of zinc are often seen as white spots on the nails, a low immunity, poor stress control, anger, slow wound healing, premature greying of hair, abnormal or absent period, and stretch marks on skin. If copper is high, you may likely be seeing low levels of zinc. The action of zinc may be blocked by excessive mercury, cadmium and copper. This means that you're likely to see low levels of zinc in smokers due to cadmium excess. Zinc is essential for fertility in males and females.

Signs and symptoms of zinc deficiency are:
- **poor growth at puberty**
- **white spots on fingernails, brittle nails**
- **microbial infections**
- **poor stress control**
- **dermatitis, eczema, dry skin, tinea, thrush, stretch marks**

* **early greying of hair**
* **poor wound healing, recurrent infections**
* **stretch marks on skin**

Supplement zinc in the diet with foods such as:
* **milk**
* **beef**
* **liver**
* **herring**
* **oysters**
* **herring**
* **ginger**
* **sunflower seeds**
* **yeast**
* **pork**
* **pumpkin seeds**

Vitamin B6 and Pyrroles

The presence of pyrroles seen as a mauve shade in the urine represents inborn errors in pyrrole chemistry which results in significant depletions on levels of vitamin B6 and zinc.

Carl Pfeiffer discovered that psychotic patients in 1970s had a mauve shade to their urine. Pfeiffer reported that more than 20% of schizophrenics had high mauve factor known as hydroxyhemopyrillone (HPL), also called pyroluria. Nutrients like B6 and zinc were essential to normalise mauve factor levels and alleviate mental health symptoms.

Often clients with depression and other mental health disorders demonstrate an abnormal production of a group of chemicals called pyrroles (pyroluria). Pyrroles rob the body of certain nutrients that need to be supplemented. The symptoms of excess urinary kryptopyrroles first manifest themselves as behavioural abnormalities. Although children tend to be more easily diagnosed than adults, the signs are consistent: poor tolerance of physical and emotional stress, mood swings, depression, and sensitivity to light, noise and other tactile sensitivities. Later symptoms can range from severe depression to chronic schizophrenia. Accompanying physical symptoms can include pain, seizures, even complete physical debilitation.

Pfeiffer, who was one of the initial investigators of mauve, treated more than one thousand high-mauve patients with vitamin B6 and zinc with very positive results. Symptom improvement with these supplements can be experienced in patients in as little as 2 days and mauve levels have been observed to decrease by as much as 50% after 1 month of treatment.[62]

Elevated levels of pyrrole are seen in families with a history of mental health conditions. It is indicative of poor methylation status. Supplementation with activated vitamin B6, biotin together with zinc and omega-6 oils are primary cofactors required to normalise pyrrole levels.

Elevated pyrroles are seen in people with high inner tension, depression, fruity body odour, explosive temper, emotional mood swings, poor short-term memory, and frequent infections. Pyroluriacs are easily identified by their inability to tan, poor dream recall, abnormal fat distribution, and sensitivity to light and sound.

Nutrients and Mood

Copper is a necessary cofactor for the synthesis of adrenal hormones from Dopamine. Dopamine is derived from two amino acids, namely tyrosine and phenylalanine. These amino acids are constituents of protein, and together with iron and folic acid, can manufacture dopamine.

Good neurotransmitter function requires sufficient reuptake at the synapse. The neurotransmitters are sucked up to the pre-synapse like a vacuum cleaner with the assistance of essential transporter proteins. The importance of the transporter proteins at the cell membrane determines how neurotransmitters are functioning at the synapse. The rate of production or inhibition of these proteins is dependent on specific nutrients.

Prozac is an example of a SSRI used for depression. From a chemical standpoint, we need amino acids, l-tryptophan and vitamin B6 to convert to active 5HTP to synthesise serotonin. A methylation cofactor called SAMe is equally important to inhibit gene expression of serotonin transporters, thereby increasing serotonin activity. Supplementation of vitamin B6, 5-HTP, SAMe and St John's wort are useful in enhancing synthesis of endogenous serotonin.

The dominant factor in depression is reuptake of neurotransmitters where the particular neurotransmitter is sucked back up to the original brain cell. This could happen if there are insufficient receptors to accept the neurotransmitter. This process happens at the presynaptic membrane where transporter protein molecules act as a conduit for returning brain chemicals. The transporter proteins are very powerful at the membrane regulating the output and input of neurotransmitters. These transporter proteins may be up- or down-regulated by certain nutrients. For example, in the absence of vitamin B6, genetic variation may express and will be indicative of undermethylation. The result of undermethylation is reduced serotonin activity typically seen in depression.

On the other hand, overmethylation may be seen in excessive dopamine activity and a tendency for anxiety, panic and paranoid schizophrenia.

Methylation

Methylation is a simply donation of methyl groups necessary for life. It can mean the difference between life and death or health and disease. Very simply analogised, we are carbon! If we burn our body, then compress it, we may become a diamond! It's the carbon footprint thing in the body! So what's so special about shifting a methyl group around?

Methylation can switch the genes on or off and is one of the body's most important chemical process underpinning every part of your physiology. It is simply the donation of methyl groups or CH_3 chemical compounds that regulate the levels of homocysteine, an inflammatory marker. Blocks in the methylation cycle can be associated with a lack of methyl donors like vitamin B6, B12, folic acid, TMG or other cofactors.

Methyl donors are added to specific elements of DNA, our gene markers and proteins that keep them physiologically active. Methylation is responsible for making, maintaining, and repairing DNA, your genetic code.

The term undermethylation is usually associated with the lack of methylation factors. Undermethylators tend to be depressed, or OCD due to a low serotonin activity. They also tend to have low calcium, magnesium vitamin B6 and methionine levels. They tend to benefit from medications that enhance serotonin levels like SSRIs but side effects are common.

A more natural approach is to directly correct the underlying problem using SAMe, methionine, calcium, and magnesium, amongst others. Although most undermethylated patients thrive on folates, supplements of folates must be avoided for patients whose problems are dominated by low activity at serotonin receptors. Folic acid, folinic acid, and methylfolate can reduce serotonin or dopamine neurotransmission by an epigenetic mechanism. Poor reaction to folate supplementation in any form requires assessment of MTHFR gene. Expression of MTHFR gene will reveal the need for methylating factors.

Signs of undermethylation:
* **OCD**
* **seasonal allergies**
* **high libido**
* **sparse body hair**
* **poor pain tolerance**
* **addictive tendencies**
* **lots of tears and saliva**
* **chronic depression**
* **sparse body hair**
* **being strong willed**
* **competitive in work or sports**

An undermethylator will benefit from supplementation with vitamin C, zinc, vitamin B6, vitamin E, methionine, SAMe, magnesium and calcium.

Sufferers of anxiety and depression may present with excessive activity of dopamine, noradrenaline and serotonin receptors. They may be overmethylators as they typically have high dopamine levels and a tendency for anxiety and paranoia. They have a genetic tendency to be very depressed in folates and other B vitamins.

Signs of overmethylation:
* **food and chemical sensitivities**
* **low motivation**

- * **low libido**
- * **antihistamine intolerance**
- * **high anxiety**
- * **upper body pain**
- * **dry eyes and mouth**
- * **sleep disorders**
- * **adverse reactions to SSRIs, SAMe, methionine**
- * **seasonal allergies**
- * **hirsutism**

Overmethylators would benefit from supplementation that will reduce activity of dopamine and noradreanaline with vitamin C, folic acid, manganese, vitamins B12 and B3, and vitamin E. Overmethylators should strictly avoid supplements containing copper, methionine, and nutrients that could aggravate anxiety and depression.

Genetic Lottery

We may exhibit traits of both parents at a physical and more often personality trait. We may even be born with tendencies for clinical depression, ADHD or schizophrenia. MTHFR is one on many gene markers that can reveal methylation defects associated with mental health disturbances.

The dominant factor is the epigenetic difference in brain chemistry.

People with genetic polymorphisms may be born with tendency for abnormal levels of key nutrients for brain chemistry synthesis. Note that the oversupply of nutrients can lead to epigenetic overload and nutrient deficiencies. Some people react to taking B-group vitamins for this reason.

Correlations Between Nutrients and Methylation

Wondered why some patients respond well to an SSRI for depression whereas others would react strongly to the point of suicide ideation? When a doctor prescribes SSRIs for depression without consideration of biochemical imbalance and genetic makeup or methylation status, a guessing game might be played.

Overmethylators don't do well with SSRIs whereas undermethylators do well. Methylating cofactors like vitamin B6 and folic acid play such a vital role in alleviating mental health conditions and have the potential to enhance the effectiveness of prescription medication if used appropriately. It is for this reason that assessment of methylation and nutrient imbalance is measured and balanced in line with other prescriptive therapies.

A lack of a simple vitamin like B6 has the potential to deplete serotonin but also convert serotonin to more toxic elements like kyneurate or quinollate. Serotonin normally is metabolised for inactivation to 5HIAA. These toxic elements are reflective in side effects as seen with SSRI supplementation.

Dopamine is made from two amino acids – tyrosine and phenylalanine – together with iron and folate. If there is a methylation defect, the capacity of the body to produce your reward neurotransmitter, even if the protein requirement is present, may be compromised.

Noradrenaline is made from dopamine. Copper and vitamin C play a vital role in the conversion. There is so much hype about too much copper and its deleterious effects. Noradrenaline requires methylation to convert to adrenaline.

Nutrients like zinc and vitamin B6 are required for synthesis of GABA, the calming neurotransmitter.

Most undermethylator depressives respond well to SSRIs. A depressed patient with folate deficiency could react adversely to SSRI.

Typically, in a zinc deficient state, pyrrole disorder, undermethylation and toxic metal levels may be seen as in Asperger's syndrome, and antisocial personality disorders.

Conversely, overmethylation, folate deficiency, and high copper levels may be seen in paranoid schizophrenia.

All of these nutrient imbalances can easily be normalised with nutrients, and thus a need for antidepressants or antipsychotics may be minimised. Patients with a methionine overload due to supplementation or diet manipulation particularly in an overmethylated patient, can react adversely and worsen.

The challenge is to identify the specific overload or deficiency and to provide treatments that normalise blood and brain levels of these chemicals.

For example, SAMe can inhibit gene expression of serotonin transporter proteins and increase serotonin activity or improve depression.

90% or more of all mental health conditions can be influenced favourably by nutrient manipulation.

In essence, the specific nutrients we get from our food influence mental health.

Pfeiffer also further published on histamine deficiency (histapenia) and copper excess in paranoid schizophrenia. He treated these patients with folic acid, vitamin B12, B3 and zinc.

In contrast, histadelic patients (histamine overload) presented with delusions, and catatonic behaviours. Antihistamines, calcium and methionine were used to treat these patients.

Nutrient disorders may include:
* **being an undermethylator – low serotonin and low dopamine, fast metaboliser**
* **pyrrole disorder – low serotonin and low GABA**
* **folate deficiency – high serotonin and dopamine**
* **copper overload – high noradrenaline, anxiety**

Having researched his condition, James initiated vitamin B6 and folic acid supplementation which made him feel agitated.

What Can Nutrients Do for James?

James had a high copper and low zinc level. In addition, ceruloplasmin, the binding protein was low, indicating that copper is not bound sufficiently allowing for free excess copper to oxidise and be toxic to the body. Copper overload is responsible for anxiety.

Elevations in copper correlates with low histamine and overmethylation. Elevations in free copper is associated with depression, panic, and low libido.

His treatment protocol incorporated minerals that assist in normalising oxidation of copper. Supplementation would consist of nutrients for an overmethylator, namely, molybdenum, zinc, magnesium, manganese and vitamin C.

In addition, James had amino acids to assist in supporting ceruloplasmin production and drive down copper, namely taurine, glutamine, histidine, threonine and cysteine.

Note that James's mercury levels were elevated. It is well-known that mercury toxicity plays a role in aggravation of mental health disturbances. Chelating mercury with specific nutrients that will assist in detoxification and clearance of these heavy metals is essential.[63]

His potassium levels were low. Sodium and potassium are two minerals that work hand-in-hand with each other to ensure that the kidneys are clearing effectively, and blood pressure is maintained. Low potassium in the bloodstream often correlates with a high sodium, which can manifest as high blood pressure. In addition, if you're low in potassium you might suffer from anxiety, depression, insomnia, constipation, heart disease, kidney stones and muscle spasms. Potassium is the third most abundant mineral in the body that regulates blood pressure, water retention, muscle activity and helps eliminate toxic waste.

You could assume that a high sodium to potassium ratio indicates excess salt intake. This may not necessarily be the case since potassium deficiency can be caused as a result of taking diuretics, diarrhoea, or chronic laxative use.

James had reported elevations in mood and stabilisation of sleep with nutrient therapy. After 3 months, he considered discussing reduction of his medication with his doctor.

Are Your Key Nutrients Deficient? Take the Quiz!

Are you at risk of high pyrroles?
- ◊ **Poor stress control**
- ◊ **Oxidative damage**
- ◊ **Inner tension**
- ◊ **Severe anxiety**
- ◊ **Psoriasis**

- Tendency to stay up late
- Fruity body odour or breath
- Negative thoughts
- Delayed puberty
- White spots on finger nails
- Dry skin
- Light sensitivity
- Mauve or dark urine
- Morning nausea
- Mood swings
- Abnormal periods
- Cravings for salty or spicy foods

Are you an undermethylator?
- Chronic depression
- OCD
- High libido
- Delusions
- Calm on the outside, tense on the inside
- Headaches
- Blank minded
- Phobias
- Addictiveness
- Suicidal tendencies
- Responds well to SSRI
- Strong willed
- Low pain tolerance
- Ritual-like behaviours
- Large nose and ears

Are you an overmethylator?
- Panic
- High anxiety
- Copper overload
- Rapid speech
- High pain threshold
- Adverse reaction to SAMe, methionine

- ◊ ***Overweight tendency***
- ◊ ***Obsessions***
- ◊ ***Sleep disorder***
- ◊ ***Tinnitus***
- ◊ ***Self-mutilation***

Calculate the number of answers you've circled against the total number of possible results. If you scored more than 30% of the checklist, you may have an imbalance. It is important to investigate your body chemistry with validated functional laboratory testing. (See Chapter 15)

13

The Meditative Brain

'We are shaped by our thoughts; we become what we think. When the mind is pure, joy follows like a shadow that never leaves.' Buddha

Have you ever felt the chill in your spine or the tingling in your head when you hear that piece of music that really touches you? Remember the inherent amazing sensation when you taste or smell something that resonates with a pleasant feeling from your past? Your subconscious mind switches on and allows you to recognise and feel the bliss. All of these feelings are a state of your mind!

The Mind-Body Connection

Throughout this book, we have made reference to the gut, diet, and adrenal, hormone and neurotransmitter levels. Why on earth do we bring the mind into the equation? No amount of neurotransmission balancing, pharmaceutical composition, diet manipulation, or exercise can balance the mind without the express intention and power of the mind.

The purpose of the *Alchemy of the Mind* is to manage the mind. This requires optimisation and balance of:

* **diet**
* **lifestyle**
* **exercise**

* **adrenal function**
* **hormonal function**
* **gastrointestinal function**
* **thyroid function**
* **neurotransmitters**
* **nutrients**

How would you react if a stranger accidentally knocked a glass of red wine on your new clothes in a restaurant? The initial reaction would be annoyance and anger. What if that person was blind? You may react differently. In a moment, the blame, which is operating from your smaller self, will transform to letting go, applying attention and intention to recognise the blame. Instead you might say 'Are you okay? Can I help you?' The key is to shift the blame from the limbic dominance, transform the trapped flight-fright-freeze response to attention and recognition. It's a response from a more awakened part of your being.

A Bit About My Experience on Meditation

I guess it's time for me to tell you a bit about myself. Though I am 'sciencey' about my approach to health and healing, I am open-minded and embrace the mind-body medicine paradigms. Mind-body medicine is not new. As a matter of fact, I have been exposed to traditional, cultural medicine from an Indian and African background. Some would call it voodoo medicine, others would call it traditional. One of the oldest forms of medicine, Ayurvedic medicine was part of my upbringing. I remember castor oil in a tiny earthenware pot on the coal stoves transformed into kohl, a paste that was applied to the eyes of young babies to ward off evil spirits. Today, women use kohl as eye makeup. There are many practices within traditional and cultural medicine throughout the world that have nothing to do with pharmaceutical medicine. One of these practices within the African culture is drumming and dancing within their community or chanting mantras, breathing techniques, singing within an Indian community, which in my opinion, is mind-body medicine. In both instances, the focused attention and enjoyment of performing the practice has the capacity to transcend your mind to a sort of blissful state. Could this be meditation?

I have been exposed to a variety of energy based mind-body medicine techniques ranging from reiki, pranic healing, massage and reflexology, body scanning, energy healing, pranayama and various forms of meditation.

You know how they say 'the answer lies within you'? We all get to a crossroad at some stage of our lives. A natural reaction is to seek the answer from out there, or from others. Learning to trust the 'gut feeling' and tap into your own energies can be fine-tuned with meditation. I personally found vipassana meditation being a profound experience and enlightening for me.

Vipassana is one of India's most ancient techniques of meditation. The tradition is taught by Goenka, originally discovered by Buddha more than 2500 years ago. Vipassana meditation aims for total eradication of mental impurities transforming the meditator through self-observation to happiness and liberation. When practised regularly, one's thoughts, feelings, judgements and sensations become clearer.

The doors to mind-body medicine are many, yet the principles are simplistic and unified. Today, they have been anglicised and marketed as new innovative techniques. Managing the mind can take many faces in the mind-body medicine arena. Some of the doors you may wish to open are psychotherapy, meditation, breathing exercises, physical exercises, emotional freedom technique, neuro-linguistic programming, gestalt therapy, imago therapy, network chiropractic, the list goes on.

When you're ready to open the door – and it is essential – you will find the right mind-body practice for you. And the sole purpose of the practice is to manage the mind and raise energy vibrations.

Hierarchy of Emotions

Emotions are never static, the change all the time! Being in love is a beautiful emotion. After a while in the relationship, do you still have the same intensity of emotion?

Mourning the loss of a loved one elicits emotions of pain, blame, regret, and fear. As time wears on, the intensity and nature of that emotion transforms to acceptance, worry or sadness. The pain of loss changes in nature with time or with therapy intervention.

Recognising and feeling negative emotions and allowing them to pass with acceptance allows you to slowly and consistently move up the hierarchy of emotions. Meditation, counselling and psychotherapy are some of the many tools of assisting in raising vibrations of emotions. Heavy emotions are fear and grief. The primary purpose of undergoing therapy or using mind-body tools are to raise the emotions to love and joy.

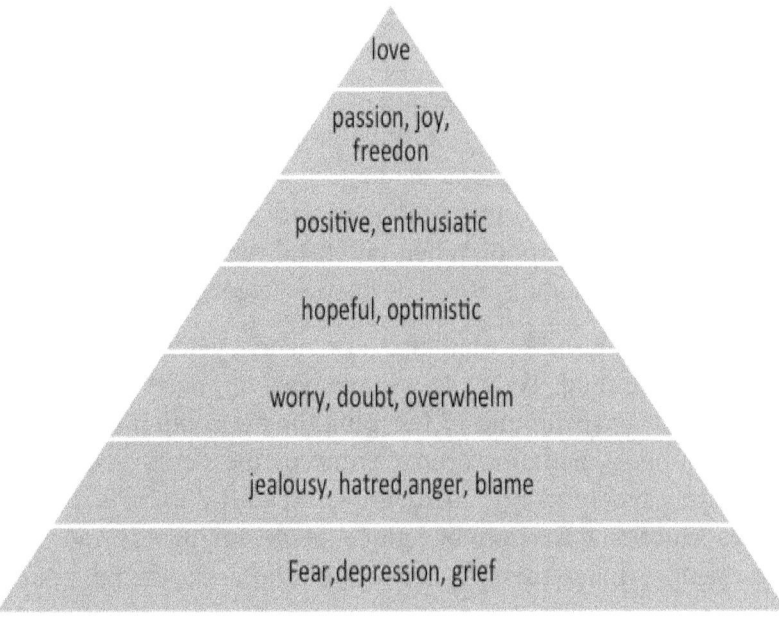

Psychotherapy, meditation and mind-body medicine plays a vital role in mental health today. In recent years, there has been a burgeoning interest in integration of Western psychotherapy techniques and Eastern meditative traditions. Versions of meditation have had their roots in ancient Buddhism and Indian medicine for thousands of years, traditionally focusing on attainment of enlightenment. Sceptics will advocate a specific form of psychotherapy against another and meditators will do the same.

True management of the mind involves an integration of all mind-body medicine techniques. Some may not wish to regurgitate their past history, or blame their parents for their misdemeanours. Some may prefer the positive thinking slant, and some would prefer to meditate. One size does not fit all. It is essential for the seeker of ultimate mind management to open the door of mind-body medicine, and find the right practice. The key is a regular practice of any modality within the mind-body medicine paradigm that suits you.

There are two types of suffering, mainly physical and psychological. Our thoughts are focused on these two areas of suffering. When you are able to tap into the space between both types of suffering, you are embracing meditation.

We use our five senses to perceive the outside world, to touch, feel, smell, hear and see. Tons of activities are being performing right within the body. The pulse and heart beats, the colon undergoes peristalsis, the blood flows, and neurons are rapidly-firing. Have you felt these actions within the body? Meditation allows you to perceive these activities and the energy flow throughout the body. It's a bit like recognising the smile in your heart or feeling the sensations in your hand inside out!

Is Mindful Awareness a Brain Thing?

> *'Mindfulness involves consciously bringing awareness to your here-and-now experience with openness, interest and receptiveness.' The Happiness Trap; Dr Russ Harris*

When something magical happens to you, the subjective sensation of exhilaration or harmony is a state of internal integration of the openness in the brain, which creates an infinite potential. Mindfulness is a state of paying attention, a state of shifting the gear in the basal ganglia of the brain to start to feel the internal world.

Mindfulness meditation was popularised by Jon Kabat-Zinn in 1979 and is now recommended by doctors today. The technique uses both breathing awareness and scanning the energy body by focusing the attention on inhalation, exhalation and the physical body from top to toe.

Mindfulness meditation has emerged as a powerful, evidence-based tool for enhancing psychological health and is now being accepted in conventional medicine. It has been proven in a wide range of clinical disorders, including chronic pain, anxiety disorders, depression, PTSD, OCD, substance abuse, and borderline personality disorder.

Mindfulness is like taking the brain to the gym. The specific brain mechanisms have been identified at the anterior cingulate in the brain. The anterior cingulate can shift the mind gear into introspection. Changing this focus of attention is an exercise for the prefrontal area. We build the prefrontal cortex to shift the gears to create an integrated state of neural balance. Mindful awareness is the first domain of neural integration, so you can focus attention to change brain function. One can use the mind to change the structure and the functioning of the brain.

The Benefits of Mindfulness

Practising mindfulness helps to:
* **be fully present, here and now**
* **safely experience unpleasant thoughts**
* **become aware of what you're avoiding**
* **become more connected to yourself, to others and to the world around you**
* **increase self-awareness**
* **become less reactive to unpleasant experiences**
* **learn the distinction between you and your thoughts**
* **have more direct contact with the world, rather than living through your thoughts**
* **learn that everything changes (that thoughts and feelings come and go like the weather)**
* **have more balance, less emotional volatility**
* **experience more calm and peacefulness**
* **develop self-acceptance and self-compassion**

Mindfulness and Therapy

Psychotherapy

Psychotherapy is a range of treatments that can help mental health problems, emotional challenges and psychiatric disorders. Conventional accredited therapy used extensively in the public health systems are CBT and DBT, forms of psychotherapy.

Psychotherapy is sometimes called the 'talking' treatment because it uses communication, understanding, guidance rather than medication. The focus is on the wider context of relationships with yourself and people around you.

Types of Psychotherapy

Behavioural therapy

The approach is to enhance positive experiences, changing undesirable to desirable responses in behaviour.

Cognitive therapy

The approach is changing the belief systems of thoughts like 'I am useless' or 'I am fearful' or 'I blame that person for this thing'. Cognitive behavioural therapy (CBT) combines cognition and behaviour to address both thoughts and actions.

Dialectical behaviour therapy

Dialectical behaviour therapy (DBT) is a therapy aimed at treating individuals with self-harm behaviours, such as self-cutting, suicidal thoughts and attempts. Many clients with these behaviours meet criteria for borderline personality disorder (BPD).

Acceptance and commitment therapy

The goal of acceptance and commitment therapy (ACT) is to create a rich and meaningful life, while accepting the pain that inevitably goes with it.

Interpersonal therapy

An approach to identify relevant emotions, where they come from, triggers of negative reactions and to resolve them through structured communication.

Family therapy

The approach is to incorporate cognitive and behavioural therapy with interpersonal relationships within the family context.

Group therapy

The approach is to help people who may feel a sense of isolation because of the issue at hand. Participation within a group can facilitate improvement and offer a rewarding experience.

Psychodynamic therapy

The approach is an insight orientated therapy focusing on deep-seated causes of behaviour. There are a wide range of associated psychotherapy techniques that have proven to be beneficial for mental health disorders.

Gestalt therapy

Delves into the philosophical underpinnings of psychotherapy training exploring the experiential world of people and understanding the attention to awareness through a process of enquiring into emergent experiences.

Ericksonian

Dr Erikson's unique approach is predominantly uncoupling conscious effort and reorganising unconscious change in mental and physical processes. The principle is to create an unconscious condition for change, then the change happens naturally.

Freudian

Classical Freudian psychoanalysis focuses on the resolution of unconscious conflicts; it is generally an 'insight' therapy, where the client is expected to spontaneously heal themselves when the contents of the unconscious are made conscious.

Inner child

The therapist's focus is to resolve the issues that bring clients to counselling and to help them to establish or re-establish their lives as a thriving process.

Integral

Integral psychotherapy attempts to combine the techniques, research and theories from the various psychological, spiritual, scientific and medical 'wisdom' traditions.

Intensive short-term dynamic psychotherapy

The primary goal of intensive short term dynamic psychotherapy (ISTDP) is to help the patient overcome internal resistance to experiencing true feelings about the present and past.

Activity Based Therapies

Dream work

Dream work helps the dreamer work with his/her own dream images, feelings, and associations, and guides the dreamer to more fully experience, appreciate, and understand the dream.

Emotional freedom techniques

Emotional freedom techniques (EFT) has been successfully applied to treat a wide range of emotional problems and issues, including anxiety, fears, phobias, trauma, grief, anger, guilt etc. It can also help improve relationships.

Art therapy

Art therapy is based on the belief that the creative process involved in the making of art is healing and life-enhancing. Creative arts therapists use arts-based processes as part of their therapeutic work with clients, to facilitate self-expression, communication, self-awareness and personal development.

Dance therapy

Dance therapy is the use of choreographed or improvised movement as a way of treating social, emotional, cognitive, and physical problems.

Emotional release

Emotional release practice offers a systematic way for people to use and recover the natural processes of emotional release, to be freer of internalised conditioning, to be more flexible and hence be more in charge of their own lives.

Music therapy

Music therapy allows persons to explore personal feelings, make positive changes in mood and emotional states, practice problem solving, and resolve conflicts leading to stronger family and peer relationships. Brain wave therapy is a form of music therapy that is distinct in rhythm and pattern to help develop new wave patterns and expand the brain to balance alpha, beta and gamma frequencies.

Yoga

A type of controlled breathing with roots in traditional yoga shows promise in providing relief for depression. One such form of yogic breathing called Sudarsham Kriya (SKY) has shown to be beneficial in depression. In this study of 45 hospitalised depression patients, 67% using SKY breathing techniques went into remission compared to those receiving ECT or antidepressant therapy.[64]

Is Meditation a Buzz Word?

Meditation is a means of transforming the mind. The practice of meditation encourages developed focused attention, clarity, emotional positivity and overall calm. Over the millennia, countless meditation practices have been developed and have proven scientifically to be extremely beneficial to each and every one of us.

Meditation is a form of deconditioning the mind by spontaneous recognition and allowing yourself to be in the present. We get caught up in our egoic mind by believing the negativity as 'I am not lovable' or 'I am in pain': it is a stuck recorder playing in the background of your mind. You must be able to recognise the pain! When you name that pain or negativity and communicate with that fear, you will start to reconnect so that it does not control you. The fear starts to take the limbic experience that has hijacked you and reconnects with the frontal cortex. When we are stressed and distressed, we lose connection with the frontal cortex and can no longer integrate with mindfulness. Recognise the nature, intensity, duration, and location of the pain to allow for re-establishment of communication with the brain.

We get ourselves so caught up in meditation. Meditation is not just a thing to do – it is a state of being.

A 1985 study published in the BMJ showed that yoga and meditation were effective in treating bronchial asthma. However, there are very few respiratory units that use meditation.[65]

Meditation has been shown to be a valuable tool in the management of:
* **hypertension**
* **cancer**
* **substance abuse**[66]
* **psoriasis**[67]

Meditation: 'Gladdening' the Mind

We often think of meditation as a serious thing to do. It feels too hard to sit still while the mind chatters away. 'I don't have time to sit still.' Or 'I have heaps of things to get done!'

Meditation allows you to gladden the mind. Thoughts are usually allocated to events of the past 'he said that', 'how dare she say that' or events of the future 'fearful of what will happen'. How often do you allocate time to be here right now?

An easy way to introduce focused attention in preparation for meditation is by allowing all your senses to be switched on whilst sipping a cup of tea. Pay attention to the smell, taste and feel of the cup in the hand. As you sip, smell and feel the explosion of tea in the mouth, feel it travelling down and truly experience drinking tea. It's quite magical!

Energy flows where the attention goes. When energy flows, the brain has a chance to rewire, change and repair neural pathways and tension. Energy flow has the power to actually change the structure and function of the brain. This means that a shift in attention to the here and now can still the mind and help you be in the moment. It allows us to shift the biochemistry of fear and anxiety to the biochemistry of stability and focused attention. Change the state of the mind by quieting the mind and then noticing just what is there in the moment. To recognise the discomfort and really feel the pain starts the travels through management of the mind, getting underneath to really touch the emotion and allow it to pass. The sustained practise of meditation as a habit, is beneficial when managing the mind.

One cannot tap into the potential of healing with the mind if you don't open the capacity to centre and ground through meditation.

Vibrations of Emotion

The human mind has great power over the body. If you can control your mind, you have a much better chance of staying healthy. If you train your mind, your body will follow. No medicine can heal your body the way your mind can.

You have probably already experienced the mind-body connection. You would have experienced this over and over again throughout your life. If you are angry, you will feel it in your body as tension, jaws clenching, heart beat increasing, or sweating. This is the negative energy. It also works for the positive energy, like when in a state of love or excitement.

When you have heavy emotions like fear, anger or shame, you vibrate at low frequencies. Feelings like love, joy and peace vibrate at high, uplifting frequencies. Your energy frequency not only affects your physiology but also those around you.

We spend much time being harsh on ourselves. Think of all the energy you spend on hating yourself, begrudging how you look, or feel perhaps when unwell. Instead, think of how much better you could feel if you took that energy and invested it in your body, taking care of it and loving it.

Remember when you cut your finger whilst preparing dinner? Your nervous system sends information throughout the body, and your entire body is flooded with chemicals in reaction to the pain you feel in your finger. When the information reaches your brain, it activates different parts of your brain. For example, the thalamus registers the trauma and sends the information on to the sensory cortex. In the sensory cortex, the information is interpreted as pain and it moves onto the next stage in the system, the motor cortex. The motor cortex sends the interpreted information 'I feel pain' to the thalamus, which sends the information throughout the body so that it can react to pain. All this happens in a matter of microseconds.

Harnessing the power of your brain is essential for health. The mind already knows that it can heal itself. You would relate to a person recovering from a disease when the doctors have declared no cure. Those that heal themselves, have being able to transform their mind to assist healing of the body.

Practical tools of awareness expansion are many and may include:

- **Belief in yourself can assist in healing, much like prayer.**
- **Find the right support with appropriate medical support.**
- **Listen to your body and your intuition. No one knows your body better than you do.**
- **Find the root cause of your illness. You need to figure out what is causing your body's self-healing mechanisms to stop working. When you have an emotional block, you're triggering your body's stress response presenting as symptoms. For every physical illness there is a corresponding emotional link.**
- **Take action! If the job or partner you have is causing stress, take action to rectify the stress rather than endure the pain.**
- **Surrender your attachments to the outcomes. Trust in the universal energy to assist you in line with all your treatment protocols.**

Louise Hay, author of *You Can Heal Your Life* believes that every physical ailment has a corresponding emotion root cause.

For example:

- **Addictions can mean fear, running from yourself or not knowing how you love yourself.**

* **Pain means feeling unloved or holding back love.**
* **Depression can mean a feeling of anger or hopelessness.**

Of course, the jury is out on its correlations. Your body has the potential to trigger an emotional response in line with physical symptoms.

Meditation Techniques

Meditation techniques may vary but the end is the same, a sense of focused attention and connecting with the self. Some prominent meditation techniques include the following.

Transcendental meditation

Transcendental meditation (TM) founded by Maharishi Mahesh Yogi was first popularised by the Beatles. It uses a mantra or a series of Sanskrit words to assist with focus and attention.

In a 1989 study researchers examined the effects of three relaxation techniques on 478 residents with an average age of 81 in 73 retirement homes. After 3 months those in the relaxation group bad a reduction in systolic blood pressure (140 down to 125 mmHg) and had improved memory. After 3 years, none of those in the TM group had died while in the control group, two thirds had.[68]

Primordial sound meditation

This is a silent practice that uses a mantra. A mantra is a vibrational sound you repeat to enter a deeper state of awareness.

Zen meditation

A seated meditation emphasises the attainment of enlightenment and personal insight by being in the present.

Kundalini meditation

Involves specific yoga practice tools to open the seventh chakra or kundalini.

Breathing Techniques

Breath is an involuntary action. Who would think that breath can detoxify the body or balance the left and right brain? Rhythmic control of breath has been shown to benefit your mind and health.

Relaxation and management of stress

Breathing techniques encourages quietening of the mind so you can focus your energy where you want it to go – on the tennis court or golf course, or in the office. Breath work encourages positive thoughts, self-acceptance and self-confidence and cleanses the body. It can be ideal to 'still the mind' in times of stress.

The spiritual benefits

The spiritual benefits of breathing techniques include the building of awareness of the body and of emotions, of being aware of the world around us, and the needs of others and increased empathy with nature. Breathing techniques promote interdependence between mind, body and spirit and helps you live the concept of 'oneness'.

How controlled breathing works

Inhalation is the intake of oxygen in the air and vital divine energy necessary for life. Vital energy permeates the entire universe and what we inhale and exhale is only a fragment of it.

Pranayama is an ancient Indian art of breathing that has been shown to improve physiology and energy of the body.

Every breath we take alters the physiology at a cellular level. Our breath feeds arteries, veins and internal organs with a medium for essential food, energy and oxygen. The veins collect the gross elements from the body, take them to heart and then to the lungs, which throws the useless material like carbon-dioxide and other toxins out of the body by the act of exhalation.

Breath allows the neuro-endocrine system to balance limbic-hypothalamus- pituitary-adrenal systems. Controlled breathing can effectively assist in stabilising stress hormones like cortisol, prolactin, adrenaline and noradrenaline.

Breathing techniques arouse the internal energy by boosting beta endorphins and encephalin levels, which can alleviate pain.

Breathing techniques and practices are marketed for a variety of conditions like Buteyko for asthma, specific conditions like liver detoxification, and weight loss or as part of religious customary rituals.

Your brain gym

We take our body to the gym! Let's take the brain to the gym through breath work and meditation.

Pranayama breathing is best practised for 10 to 45 minutes each morning. Sit upright in a comfortable position either on a chair or on the floor, and ensure that the spine and neck is kept straight and stable.

Focus *only* on your breath visualising in-breath nourishing with vital universal energy and out-breath expelling all the toxins of the mind and body.

Start with 2 minutes of each exercise daily increasing slowly to 5 minutes of each exercise.

Breathing exercises which will offer immediate benefits include some of the following.

Humming bee

Brain fog? This exercise is brilliant for clearing the head, and awakening the mind. It's ideal to perform this breathing exercise when you feel flat and tired. It was once said, 'It feels like a cobweb brush just cleared all the woolly brain fog, I feel clear and fresh in my head.'

Close ears with thumb, index finger on forehead, and remaining three fingers shutting the eyes lightly. Switch off the distracting senses in preparation for this exercise.

Breathe in deeply, and as you exhale, breathe out through the nose while humming like a bee. Ensure that you hum loudly and forcefully. Visualise the activation of various parts of the brain. This exercise clears the headspace and awakens the senses.

Panting dog

Breathe in through both the nostrils forcefully, till the lungs are full, abdomen is extended, and diaphragm is stretched. Extend your tongue like a panting dog, and breathe out forcefully through your mouth. It's important to ensure that you breathe out forcefully as the abdomen is contracted upon exhalation. It could feel like you're being punched in the stomach. In this way, you are whipping the stomach, and panting loudly and forcefully though the mouth.

This exercise is useful to regulate bowel function, digestion, and purify the blood by increasing oxygenation to the cells, and detoxifying the body using your breath.

Alternate nostril breathing

Sitting straight, focusing only on your breath, position the right hand thumb on the right nostril, three fingers on left nostril and index finger on the forehead. Visualise your in-breath travelling from right brain to left brain and down left side of body and vice versa upon exhalation.

With right hand in position (thumb released) breathe in through the right nostril to the count of two, close both nostrils by holding the breath, and then exhale by releasing right nostril. Alternate opening each nostril with each breath.

Prana breathed in through the left nostril represents energy of the moon, which symbolises peace, and has a cooling effect. Close the right side nostril with the right-hand thumb. Inhale slowly through the left nostril till the lungs are filled. Then close the left nostril with the second and third fingers. Open the right nostril and exhale through it. Repeat this exercise slowly in the beginning, and with practice, increase the speed.

When you are able to practise this exercise for a long time, inhale with as much force as is possible for you, then exhale forcefully.

It is said that this breathing exercise when practised regularly will awaken the kundalini.

Repeat this exercise increasing counts to three, then four, and so on.

This exercise balances left and right brain. The same principals are used in components of Buteyko breathing and is useful in asthma, sinusitis, rhinitis and COPD.

If you choose to open the mind-body medicine door, embrace what feels right for you, stick with the exercise consistently on a daily basis for at least 30 days without fail. If it doesn't do anything for you within that time, try another exercise.

14

Is the Brain a Meaning Organ?

We will never be able to fully understand the complexities of the brain. A typical adult brain has a hundred billion brain cells and an average of 1000 synaptic connections per brain cell. Every emotion, be it love, passion, hatred, anger – and every thought – is triggered by special chemicals called neurotransmitters. In this book we have focused on the dominant neurotransmitters. However, there are thousands of neurotransmitters, some of which have not been identified. We are not made with a lifetime supply of brain chemicals when we're born. Instead the brain, together with other organs, including the gut, act as a chemical factory that continuously produces neurotransmitters throughout our lifetime.

The brain is a memory and meaning organ. When you hear the word 'rose', it activates some part of the cortex, a point of prior learning in the brain recognising that any rose that you see afterwards is called a rose and not something else. Brain connections are made every time you form a new memory.

Humans are blessed with a prefrontal cortex, the point of mindfulness and intellect. Despite the rapidly expanding amount of research on the brain, the mind and consciousness will never know the whole story. Our body stops growing in our late teens; cells replace each other throughout our lives. As an example, red blood cells are replaced every 14 days. The brain doesn't ever stop growing. The concept of neuronal plasticity is evidence of the fact that the brain can repair and rewire itself.

The interest in neuroscience and the progressively increasing incidence of mental illness has been reframed into a form of hypermania. It's like a juicer that's out of control with no off button. Your thoughts and actions become scrambled and not logical, which leads you to be irrational and what others would call 'something wrong with you'.

When we talk about the brain, it is anything but one-dimensional or simplistic. The brain is an organ of surreal complexity, and we understand just a fraction of it. There are about 100 billion neurons in the cortex and 100 trillion synapses that make up all the connections. We're trying to figure out this complex machine that does extraordinary processing way beyond any computer. Terms like *mind, consciousness, intellect*, and *brain* leaves much to be debated.

We're starting to understand how the brain processes abnormally in illnesses like depression, OCD and post-traumatic stress. We are able to identify some of the connection differences, or some of the circuitry that is different for people with these disorders. The circuitry is called the human connectome, which reveals variation in the way the brain is wired. There are predictable patterns in brain disorders like Alzheimer's or Parkinsonism.

Technologies like electroencephalogram (EEG), quantitative EEG, MRI and CT scans are used in mental health for diagnostic purposes.

Brain Representation as a Fist

The works of a renowned professor in psychiatry, Daniel Siegel in 'minding the brain' describes the brain structure much like a clenched fist. If your thumb is folded over into a clenched fist, it can represent a simplistic model of the brain with the front of the knuckles being the frontal cortex. The back of the head is represented by the back of the hand, and the spinal cord rising from the backbone is the wrist and arm.

The frontal cortex, represented by the knuckles is pronounced in humans as opposed to animals. This area controls voluntary muscles like movement of hands and feet, and provides intellect, allowing us to plan motor actions in the physical world and enables interaction with our external environment.

The prefrontal cortex represented by the front of the knuckles is located behind the forehead, and is a point of conscious focus and attention.

The limbic region represented by the thumb has evolved significantly within the mammalian brain and is responsible for evoking emotions, motivation, and regulation. Within the limbic region, vital parts of the brain called the hypothalamus and pituitary influence the endocrine system or sex, adrenal and thyroid hormones. The limbic area also helps us create memories, emotions, and record depths of sound, colour or emotions. The amygdala is considered to be an organ of perception and conscious awareness. This organ plays a role in subconscious awareness, like when you have reacted to the 'gut feeling'. The hippocampus is an organ of perception that converts our experiences into memories, a repository for language centres or recollections.

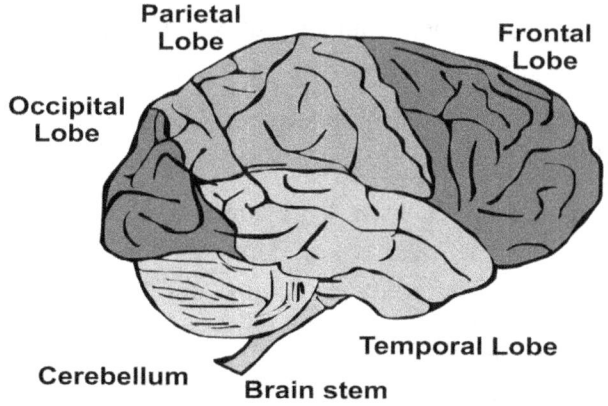

The brain stem, represented by the wrist, sends signals from the brain throughout the body. The signals allows the heart to beat, our lungs to breathe, and the skin to feel. The brain stem forms part of motivational systems that assists us to satisfy our basic needs for food, shelter and safety.

When the amygdala receives a signal of a potential accident, for example, it activates a portion of the occipital lobe which then activates the prefrontal cortex to respond to that accident. When the danger of the accident is brought to your consciousness, the flight-fright-freeze response is initiated, allowing you to react by stimulating the prefrontal cortex really quickly to get involved and figure out consciously the course of action. The brain is a wonderfully complex organ.

How do we keep generating new thoughts or memories? It happens with a process of regeneration of the brain called neurogenesis and neuroplasticity.

Neurogenesis

Neurogenesis is a process that happens in our brain to generate new brain cells every day of our lives. The brain makes 700 new neurons per day to assist us with memory, learning, and excitation. Neurons are made to improve the quality of our memory. Without these neurons, we cannot remember to find a car in a parking lot, for example. When we use drugs, even cancer drugs, alcohol, and when under chronic stress, the brain cells slow down regeneration. At this stage, the brain stops making new neurons and connections. Animals on the other hand, have a slower rate of neurogenesis, and hence fail to have the quality of intellect of a human.

Neurogenesis slows down when under stress, as we age, drink alcohol or use illicit drugs.

Neurogenesis speeds up when we learn, sleep well or have sex. It also speeds up when we eat, take antioxidants such as berries and dark chocolate. Diet therefore modulates memory and focus.

Your State Becomes Your Trait

Conscious choices of diet manifests in health. "You are what you eat." Likewise, deliberate practice of the mind is represented by the mind state which manifests as a mind trait. A mind state become a mind trait! A strong mindset may be defined as effective, focused, determined and confident. The traits which help build a strong mindset include positive and vibrant thoughts, an active physical body, knowledge and application of deep thinking, and self-discipline.

Pain, whether it be social or physical, is perceived in the prefrontal cortex. The interior world is perceived as introception, perhaps the sixth sense. Introception allows you to have mindsight, or knowing your inner world. Your mind state becomes your mind trait. If you are angry, then anger is presented in your internal world. Anger manifests physiologically as tension, palpitations, sweats and irrational behaviour. Conversely, in a state of calm, as in a meditative state, GABA is squirted from the limbic area in the prefrontal area into the amygdala. Thoughts and emotions play out a series of chemical reactions by stimulating various parts of the brain.

Neurons That Wire Together, Fire Together

Messages get sent on a microsecond basis as long as we're alive. If you touch fire, the brain sends signals for you to react immediately. Neurons send these messages in different ways.

Synaptogenesis is a process where messages are sent from one neuron to another across the synaptic cleft.

Myelinogenesis is a process of neurotransmission when messages are sent along the myelin sheath or the spindle. The myelin sheath is surrounded by a fatty layer that acts as an insulator much like the carpet around a rod full of fat to increase the speed of conduction. After all, the brain is 60% fat. The greater the good oil content of the brain, the faster the nerve transmission.

Neural firing is neuronal plasticity. Stimulating the brain with new activities, learning or experiences is necessary to make new neurons and change the brain.

External factors like music, the smell of chocolate or coffee, has the power to increase brain waves, which triggers satisfaction or relaxation.

Some fun facts about the brain:
* **The brain uses about 20% of the total oxygen and blood in your body.**
* **Sexual appetite and libido starts in the brain.**
* **Taste receptors are found in the brain. This is why you salivate when you desire specific foods or drinks.**
* **Lack of oxygen in the brain for 5 to 10 minutes results in permanent brain damage.**

Energy and Information Flow

As we examine the architecture of the brain, the mind determines how information flows to parts of the brain or the muscles for action. The brain has the ability to transition through various frequencies to allow for vital functions like taking on a task, thinking or sleeping.

The function of the mind is energy and information flow, ideally with compassion, love and feeling. The circuits of the brain become engaged by stimulation of the senses from people or the environment through a flow of energy and information. Positive emotions allows for a conscious opportunity to ride out any storm or react proactively to a fight-flight-freeze response. When in a reactive state, the brain signals for fight and fright and a need for action. This means that you're unable to be receptive or open to another. The emotional distress causes chaos and disintegration of the mind.

On the other hand, when in a calm state, an attitude of receptivity open up the opportunity for the brain to send signals of relaxation of facial muscles, vocal chords, normalise blood pressure, all of which turns on good feelings, social engagement and connection.

Feeling is that energy that forms with shifts of emotion, like recognising and old friend in a crowd. Emotions are integrated shifts of various parts of the brain as we react or connect our thoughts.

Brainwaves

The brain is a social and meaning organ. Energy and information flows with different types of electrical patterns or brainwaves across the cortex. The brainwaves can be observed with an electroencephalogram (EEG) and each brainwave has a purpose and assists in information flow.

Different brainwaves may be dominant through different parts of the day depending on the state of consciousness you're in.

There are five main brainwaves that have been identified. For example, *gamma* waves are involved in rapid eye movement (REM) sleep. *Beta* waves means a state of wakefulness, thought and logical thinking. Drinking stimulating coffee or alcohol may activate beta waves. *Alpha* waves assists in being calm and relaxed. Playing music stimulates alpha wave activity and can assist in synchronising the brain and aid insomnia. *Theta* waves are connected to deep emotions. A meditative or semi-hypnotic state is a theta state. *Delta* waves are the slowest waves associated with deep and healing sleep.

Interpersonal Brain Connections

Ever stopped to smell the roses? Imagine feeling the crunch of autumn leaves under the feet! When neurons are activated, they secrete BDNF (brain derived neurotrophic factor), which enhances the capacity to stimulate more synaptic connections. The nucleus bacillus is activated with concentrated mass squirts of acetylcholine (Ach), a neuro modulator. Neuromodulators are much like a medium through which neurotransmitters can fire across the neuro synaptic cleft. When neuromodulators like Ach, phosphatidylserine, inositol, and the good oils are in abundance, the action of neurotransmitters is optimised. As the membrane becomes bathed in Ach, neural firing stimulates concentration, focus and attention.[69]

Focused attention stimulates neural integrative firing, which allows you to feel the vibration, to feel the harmony as if the entire choir is in sync and in harmony. This harmony is a state of subjective sensation and integration.

Integration is the relationship between mindfulness and compassion. Meditation is a practice of powerfully harnessing the attention. It improves immunity, prevents relapses, improves anxiety, assists with PTSD, and drug abuse.

Fatigue and lethargy is a state of living in an insanely productive and erratic consciousness. We get caught up in a rat race and are unable to discriminate the wisdom and time to nurture inner consciousness. The real power is to dedicate the time to stand, explore the unknown of your insecurities and enjoy the moment.

Neuronal Plasticity

The brain keeps developing until you die.

Depression in essence is inhibited neuronal plasticity. The brain gets stuck. Freud in 1885 postulated in his law of association that neurons that fire together, wire together.

Neuronal plasticity can be enhanced with exercise, sleep, nutrition and water. So when you activate your attention, you activate the superior temporal cortex. Neural transmission activates the genes to produce proteins to get new neurons to grow – and this is called neuronal firing.

The brain changes itself!

15

Don't Guess! Assess and Address

Why Test?

Functional medicine involves identifying core imbalances that affect the brain and body network. There is no separating the brain and the body – what affects the body affects the brain.

Treatment should be based on careful history taking, questionnaires, physical exam, targeted laboratory testing and customised therapy

All of the following chemicals may affect moods, memory and cognitive processes:

* **amino acids – especially tryptophan, tyrosine and phenylalanine**
* **antioxidants, vitamins and minerals**
* **C-reactive protein, interleukins and various inflammatory biomarkers**
* **cortisol and DHEA(s)**
* **formiminoglutamic acid (FIGLU), methylmalonic acid (MMA) – folate and B12 metabolites**
* **heavy metals and/or environmental pollutants**
* **histamine**
* **kryptopyrroles (mauve factor)**
* **MTHFR and methylation co-factors**
* **neurotransmitter metabolites – 5-HIAA, VMA, VMA, DOMA, DOPAC, MHPG, DHPG**

* neurotransmitters – GABA, glutamate, dopamine, serotonin, adrenaline and noradrenaline
* thyroid, sex and adrenal hormones

Don't Guess! Test, Treat and Target Tailor

After all, your biology is in your biochemistry!

No two fingerprints are the same. We are as unique as our biochemistry. We cannot apply 'one size fits all' treatment approach. Assessments therefore need to be individualised.

Core areas of assessment could include:
* **hormonal, adrenal and thyroid imbalances**
* **neurotransmitter imbalances**
* **oxidation-reduction imbalances, mitochondrial dysfunction**
* **detoxification, neurotoxicity, and biotransformation imbalances**
* **immune imbalances (cytokine hypothesis)**
* **inflammatory imbalances**
* **digestive, absorptive, and microbiological imbalances**
* **structural and membrane imbalances**
* **psychological and spiritual equilibrium**

More specifically, I believe that assessment of mental health can be achieved through accredited diagnostic criteria (DSM) and lab testing.

Baseline testing should at a minimum constitute assessment of:
* **adrenals**
* **neurotransmitters**

Assuming that the gut, hormone levels, and diet are in check, the following lab tests would reveal all the kinks or metabolic blocks in mental health and genetic aberrations in the biochemistry.
* **Zinc and copper levels**
* **Methylation defects**
* **Pyrrole**
* **Histamine**
* **Amino acids**
* **Oxidative stress**
* **Vitamin B6**

* **Nutrient imbalances**
* **Heavy metal toxicities**
* **Environmental pollutant exposure**

Choose the Right Test

Generally, I tend to identify adrenal status and neurotransmitter profiles as a baseline to give an indication of stage of adrenal dysfunction, and the balance of excitatory and inhibitory neurotransmitters. It is essential to go upstream to identify the underlying causes of mental health disturbances. If you have gut problem, no amount of nutrient support will completely rectify mental health unless the body is able to absorb and utilise these nutrients with optimal gut health essential to mood management.

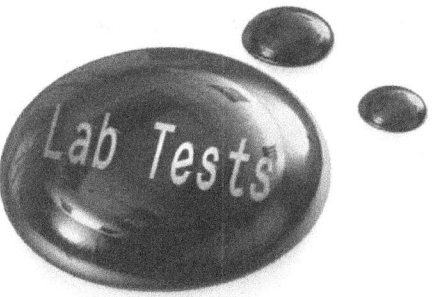

Choose the Right Sample

Most functional pathology tests can be performed in more than one tissue sample. Neurotransmitters can be measured in urine and also cerebrospinal fluid (though we definitely would not want the latter!).

All tests can be performed in one of many tissue samples. Cortisol, as an example is measured four times in a day in saliva. It is not feasible to have blood drawn every 4 hours.

Lab tests can be performed on blood, plasma, blood spot, urine, saliva, stool, buccal swab and hair.

What Is Functional Pathology?

Functional pathology tests are used to investigate biochemical, nutritional, metabolic and hormonal status that may be cause illness.

The results provide essential information to assist the practitioner in the diagnosis, treatment and management of patients seeking a holistic approach to health

Most tests are designed so patients can collect specimens in the privacy of their own homes.

It's a balancing act, weighing the expense of tests with their usefulness in improving symptoms. In general, the more abnormal the results, the greater the chance for improvements after implementing therapies. Keep in mind that one approach never suits all.

Functional pathology testing provides a tool for early intervention, management and monitoring for ongoing treatment efficacy, especially when presenting with chronic unresolved symptoms and/or conditions.

Whilst an extensive range of tests are available, the tests below have been used in case studies pertaining specifically to mental health and its associated conditions.

* **Adrenal stress**
* **Neurotransmitter tests**
* **Amino acids**
* **Pyrrole**
* **Histamine**
* **Gastrointestinal tract tests**
* **Allergy/food intolerance testing**
* **Hormonal profile**
* **Thyroid testing**
* **Zinc and copper ratios**
* **Genetic diagnostic testing**
* **Nutritional profile or energy testing**

Differences Between Functional Pathology and Tests by Your Doctor

The public health system allows for a vast range of essential tests to identify disease states. Advancements in pathology have developed to incorporate tests that can identify underlying causes of disease or chemical imbalances in the body.

For example, your doctor may perform a liver test identifying the various transferase enzymes, essentially to diagnose cirrhosis of the liver. Functional pathology can measure a detailed assessment of phase 1 and 2 of liver detoxification including all the conjugation pathways. Detailed liver function reveals genetic aberrations in cytochrome enzyme pathways that affect detoxification and metabolism of food, hormones and drugs.

Mental health uses DSM criteria for diagnosis. Functional pathology uses assessment of excitatory and inhibitory neurotransmitters in a urine sample.

Ideally, conventional medicine needs to incorporate functional medicine for integrated wellness.

What Is DSM?

The conventional medicine assessment of mental health approach is the DSM model. The diagnostic and statistical manual of mental disorders (DSM) is a compilation of many questionnaires used by medical professionals to diagnose mental health. DSM uses a symptom based criteria to standardise diagnostic categories for diagnosis and treatment.

DSM is one of many diagnostic symptom-based assessment system that is used by professionals in conjunction with clinical expertise. However, DSM might be considered controversial in that the complexity of patient presentations may not be adequately summarised by the limited diagnostic codes. In addition there may be an overlap between different disorders like depression and anxiety.

Which Test Is the Right Test?

Lab tests are listed in order of priority based on what I see in clinical practice. Note that the underlying causes always needs to be assessed, and addressed as mental health is managed.

Adrenal stress

Stress is best measured in saliva. Cortisol can be measured four times in a day to track diurnal rhythms of cortisol release. The adrenal test is a four point cortisol with DHEA in a saliva DIY test. Cortisol can be measured in blood, urine and blood spot.

Neurotransmitter tests

'Happy and sad' brain chemicals are neurotransmitters that can be measured in a urine sample incorporating both inhibitory and excitatory neurotransmitters, viz. serotonin, dopamine, GABA, glutamate, dopamine, noradrenaline and adrenaline.

Amino acids

Up to 40 amino acids can be measured in urine or blood. Amino acids are building blocks of protein needed for practically every physiological process in the body from neurotransmitter production, liver detoxification to energy production. This test is helpful in assessing causes and treatments for lethargy, mood disorders, muscle weakness, vitamin deficiency, protein intolerance, inborn errors of metabolism and seizures. Many of these symptoms are caused or worsened by elevated levels of gastrointestinal yeast or bacteria.

Pyrrole

Pyrroles or mauve factor test (formerly known as kryptopyrroles) is a urinary test that analyses the level of HPL, a neurotoxic substance found in schizophrenia, autism, ADHD, alcoholism, violent offenders and other mental health disorders. High levels of the mauve factor is associated with vitamin B6 and zinc deficiencies.

Histamine

Histamine is a biologically active amine that is involved in immune responses, the regulation of the gut and acts as a neurotransmitter. Imbalances of histamine have been implicated in allergies, schizophrenia, depression, anxiety, behavioural disorders and autism. Histamine is not solely involved in allergic inflammation responses. It also has neurotransmitter-like action affecting brain chemistry. Serum levels can reflect low levels (histapenia) or high levels (histadelia) of which either can be associated with neurological problems/behaviour.

Gastrointestinal tract tests

The comprehensive digestive stool analysis (CDSA) is an advanced non-invasive diagnostic tool for assessing gastrointestinal function from the time food enters the mouth until it leaves the body through elimination. As the CDSA combines a large number of tests that evaluate the function of the gastrointestinal tract, a comprehensive picture of a patients gut health can be obtained. The analysis investigates digestion, metabolism, absorption and metabolic markers and pancreatic function. This test reports on the balance of good bugs or beneficial bacteria and the presence of bad bugs or pathological bacteria, yeast and parasites.

Allergy and food intolerance testing

Food allergy, intolerance or sensitivity is measured through immunoglobulin testing. These tests measure relative allergy to foods that may cause effects hours after ingestion. It identifies and differentiates between gluten and gliaden in wheat products and casein and whey in dairy together with fruit, vegetables, grains and protein sources.

ALCAT testing detects inflammation of white blood cells. In addition to foods, ALCAT detects allergy to food chemicals such as dyes and preservatives, moulds and environmental chemicals.

Hormone testing

Male and female hormones can be measured in saliva, blood, urine or blood spot. Sex hormones manufacture the stress hormone, cortisol, and stress hormones can cause neurotransmitter imbalances.

Hormones measured are predominantly progesterone, oestrogens, DHEA, testosterone and hormone metabolites.

Thyroid testing

Thyroid hormones can be measured in urine or blood. Thyroid dysregulation correlates with adrenal dysfunction and mental health disturbances. Thyroid hormones measured are predominantly TSH, T3, T4, reverse T3, thyroid antibodies, iodine and cofactors in thyroid hormone production.

Zinc and copper ratios

The ratio of zinc and copper plays a significant role in mental health. These minerals have profound implications in neurological and behavioural disorders and correlates with methylation status, gene mutations, MTHFR, histamine, and ceruloplasmin. This test aims to identify oxidative damage caused by copper toxicity and associated zinc deficiency.

Methylation

Methylation is identified by a gene marker, MTHFR (methyltetrahydrofolate). Methylation defects can be established with identification of methionine, folate, SAMe cycles and levels of homocysteine.

Genetic diagnostic testing

MTHFR is a marker of gene mutation for methylation function. MTHF gene plays a role in processing amino acids and underpins virtually every physiological function in the body. It requires methyl group derived from methylating donors like specific B group vitamins, folic acid and amino acids to keep homocysteine, an-inflammation marker in check.

If a gene mutation is present, it is best to measure the methylation blocks within the methylation cycle. The markers of methylation that can be measured are SAMe, SAH, tetrahydrofolate, folinic acid, methionine, homocysteine and 5MTHF.

Nutritional profile or energy testing

After fats, carbohydrates and proteins are metabolised in the gastrointestinal tract, nutrients are absorbed by the bloodstream and processed in the mitochondria of each cell to produce energy in the form of adenosine triphosphate (ATP). The process of energy production within the mitochondria is called the Krebs cycle. The metabolic blocks within the Krebs cycle reveal information about neurotransmitter function, B group vitamin insufficiency, amino acid insufficiency, urea cycle, coenzyme Q10 utilisation, fatty acid metabolism, bacterial dysbiosis, candida infestation, and methylation defects. Elevations in organic acids measured in urine can affect neurological functioning, vitamin utilisation, energy level, intestinal wall integrity, hormone utilisation and muscle function.

Heavy metal toxicity

Toxic metals are present in air, water, soil and our food supply. Normally, the immune system and liver detoxification pathways are sufficient to clear toxins. However, contamination is so pervasive in our environment, particularly lead, mercury and cadmium, contributing to a wide array of problems. Mental health problems associated with heavy metal toxicity range from neuropsychiatric disorders such as aggressive behaviour, memory loss, depression, irritability, Alzheimer's disease learning difficulties and chronic fatigue syndrome.

Heavy metals can be measured in hair, urine and blood. Hair tissue mineral analysis detects long-standing exposure of heavy metals since hair is a storage vesicle. Urine metal analysis reflects metabolic exposure of metals and minerals. Heavy metals in a blood sample detects metal toxicity that is reflective at tissue level.

Essential fatty acids

Like vitamins and minerals, essential fatty acids (EFAs) are vital to health. They are necessary for cellular membrane integrity which allows correct functioning at a base level. EFAs are also important for proper brain function. EFAs comprise omega-3, omega-6 and omega-9 found in foods and ideally should be present in the ratios of 3:2:1 simultaneously.

To Test or Not to Test?

There are many mental health screening tools available. Acknowledgement of 'there may be something wrong with my mind' is the first step. Though we all experience stress, anxiety and perhaps bouts of depression, not all of us have mental health conditions.

Recognising symptoms through appropriate screens is advisable as a starting point. Always go upstream of biochemical pathways to identify the underlying cause of mood changes. The integrative medicine approach involves identifying core imbalances that affect the brain and body network.

Take the step and feel better by balancing your brain chemistry!

Learn More

I do hope that *Alchemy of the Mind* has widened your perspective in relation to the underlying causes, treatments, and various avenues of healing the mind. It must be noted that *Alchemy of the Mind* is not a medical text upon which you can rely on for diagnosis and treatment. If you follow the basics of balancing body chemistries as explained in this book, moods can change for the better! It is imperative that diet is optimised and you have adequate sleep, exercise regularly, drink sufficient water, and eat high quality healthy food. Balance body and brain chemistries with the help of your healthcare practitioner. There is much still to be detailed that can further unravel brain chemistries, such as methylation defects, genetic polymorphisms, and the impact of environmental pollutants on the brain. Don't hesitate to find a healthcare practitioner who is knowledgeable and open-minded about pursuing a functional approach to balancing brain chemistries. Many have consulted with a variety of healthcare providers and continue to suffer.

Balance brain chemistries with *Alchemy of the Mind*!

See **www.vanitadahia.com** for further education and a deeper dig into brain chemistries!

What Next?

Congratulations on having come this far!

You probably have got to know me a little through this book. The fact that you're reading my book means that I can get to know you too. Don't panic, I cannot read your mind. If you got this far, you would probably be keen in understanding the chemistries of your mind and of your body. Are you ready to identify your biochemistry and balance it naturally?

It is quite clear that you must bring about change in the way you think in order to create happiness and vitality. Isn't it wonderful that the brain has the capacity to change? You can willingly adopt changes just through changing your thinking patterns.

How do you translate the knowledge that you have learnt into happiness? Where do you begin?

Start by finding the chapter that resonates the most with you. Use the quizzes to determine your chemical imbalances. Take the appropriate assessments.

Let's consider the following steps:
- review medical history and symptoms
- prioritise lab testing
- identify chemical imbalances
- develop a tiered treatment strategy for approximately 3 months
- further round of lab assessments to determine efficacy and fine tuning of treatment
- a tiered natural treatment strategy
- provide after-care

The focus of treatment is to identify and correct your body's chemistry. This is not a bandaid approach. Each clinical step is essential to success. The therapy approach is complex and comprehensive, and hence requires supervision of an experienced integrative healthcare professional.

Medical history and review of symptoms

An in-depth knowledge of your health, family history, and genetic polymorphisms are essential to develop a successful treatment plan for balancing brain chemistries.

Some of the factors that are necessary for establishing a medical history are:
- current medication regime
- allergies to food or medicine
- family history
- occupation
- early health issues and operations
- developmental milestones
- illnesses
- substance abuse issues
- food intolerances, sensitivities or allergies
- chemical sensitivities
- overt mental health concerns

In addition, a detailed overview of health status is recommended to include:
- a diet diary
- gut function
- hormones

* **thyroid**
* **essential fatty acids deficiencies**
* **neurotransmitter function**

Prioritise Lab Testing

I use the term prioritise purely because there are a multitude of lab assessments that can provide valuable clues and evidence of an imbalanced brain.

My approach would be to establish a basic test portfolio in combination with detailed questionnaires in order to glean as much information as possible with minimal testing. Some of the tests used routinely in mental health specifically are prioritised below.

Testing for the Mind

Identify chemical imbalances

Chemical imbalances can only be identified through validated lab testing, be it conventional or functional. Some allied health practitioners may use kinesiology, muscle testing, bio impedance testing or healing modalities to assist in identifying chemical imbalances. Some of these assessments are neither validated nor accredited with associated governing bodies and therefore should be used at your discretion.

A tiered natural treatment strategy (for approximately 3 months)

Treatment can take place in the form of prescription medication, compounded medication, targeted individualised natural therapies, herbs, homeopathic supplements, tissue salts, or diet. Don't treat yourself without professional health advice.

Our brain chemicals are made from specific nutrients, amino acids, vitamins and minerals. It is essential therefore to replenish what is missing from the body, and allow these vital brain chemicals to be naturally normalised in order to restore optimal mental health.

Why 3 months?

Cells die and are replaced throughout life. Most of the body regenerates itself in approximately 3 months. All cells have a lifespan. For example, the cells that line the gut last for 5 days, red blood cells turn over every 14 days, and bone osteoblasts up to 3 months. Of course, there are cells such as lens cells and oocytes that last a lifetime.

In practice, I have found that correcting an organ system usually simultaneously with other organ systems can address a significant number of imbalances effectively and efficiently within a 3 month period

Further round of lab assessments to determine efficacy and fine tuning of treatment

How would you know if you're getting better if you don't establish what you need or monitor the effectiveness of treatment? You might need to be very selective in retesting only certain analytes to make your journey to great mental health economically viable.

Develop a maintenance natural treatment strategy

Once one organ system is managed, it's important to go further upstream to correct any residual chemical imbalances. For example, if diet is implicated in your mood, adjustment of your diet in conjunction with optimising gastrointestinal function will assist in improved mental health.

It is very easy to regress in your treatment strategies. If you happen to follow a weight loss program, enthusiasm in the initial phases may wane in time.

The Final Word

In mental health, however, embrace all components of mood management – there are many aspects of diet and mind-body medicine to consider.

The brain is in charge of the body. Balance body chemistries to balance brain chemistries!

References

1. Journal of Religion and Health 51(3): 925–933. October 2010.
2. Cooper JR, Bloom FE, Roth RH. The Biochemical Basis of Neuropharmacology. New York: Oxford University Press, 1996.
3. T.C.Birdsall. Five HTP a clinical affective serotonin precursor, alternative medicine review three (1998). PP271–280.
4. Rada P, Avena NM, Hoebel BG. Daily bingeing on sugar repeatedly releases dopamine in the accumbens shell. Neuroscience. 2005 Jun 26.
5. Noh JS, et al. Neurotoxic and neuroprotective actions of catecholamines in cortical neurons. Experimental Neurology. 1999;159:217–24.
6. Cartford MC, Gould T, Bickford PC. A central role for norepinephrine in the modulation of cerebellar learning tasks. Behav Cogn Neurosci Rev. 2004 Jun; 3(2): 131–8.
7. Singh P, Mann KA, Mangat HK, Kaur G. Prolonged glutamate excitotoxicity: effects on mitochondriaantioxidants and antioxidant enzymes. Mol Cell Biochem. 2003 Jan; 243(1–2):139–45.
8. Cavalheiro EA, Olney JW. Glutamate antagonists: deadly liaisons with cancer. Proc Natl Acad Sci USA. 2001 May 22; 98(11): 5947–8.
9. Jordan D, et al. Endocrinology. 1979 Oct; 105(4): 975–9.
10. Nora D.et al. Dopamine drug abuse and addiction, Arch Neurol. 2007;64(11): 1575–1579.
11. Kevin M Gray et al., NAC in young marijuana users, Am J Addict. 2010 Mar 1; 19(2): 187–9.
12. Di Forti M, Iyegbe C, Sallis H, et al. Confirmation that the AKT1(rs2494732) genotype influences the risk of psychosis in cannabis users. Biol Psychiatry. 2012; 72(10): 811–816.
13. Caspi A, Moffitt TE, Cannon M, et al. Moderation of the effect of adolescent-onset cannabis use on adult psychosis by a functional polymorphism in the catechol-Omethyltransferase gene: longitudinal evidence of a gene X environment interaction. Biol Psychiatry. 2005; 57(10): 1117–1127.
14. Kenneth Blum Et al. Int. J. Environ. Res. Public Health. 2011, 8, 4425–4459.

15. NAC in cannabis dependant adolescents, Gray, KM et al., Am J Psychiatry. 2012 Aug; 169(8): 805–12.

16. Aragon, G, Graham, D, Borum, M (2016, January 10). Probiotics therapy for irritable bowel syndrome. Gastroenterol Hepato. 2010 Jan; 6(1): 39–44

17. Lyte M, Barratt, E, et al. Microbial Endocrinology: The Microbiota-Gut-Brain Axis in Health and Disease, GABA production by culturable bacteria from the human intestine. J.App Microbiol. 11, 411–417.

18. Buie, T., D.B. Campbell, et al. (2010). 'Evaluation, diagnosis, and treatment of gastrointestinal disorders in individuals with ASDs: a consensus report.' Pediatrics. 125 Suppl 1: S1–18.

19. Tang M, Ponsonby A, Orsini F, Tey D, Robinson M, Su E. Administration of a probiotic with peanut oral immunotherapy: A randomized trial.The Journal of Allergy and Clinical Immunology. 2015.

20. Diurnal patterns of salivary cortisol and cortisone output in chronic fatigue syndrome. Jerjes WK, et al. J Affect Disord. 2005 Aug; 87(2-3): 299–304.

21. Pharmacological and nonpharmacological factors influencing hypothalamic-pituitary-adrenocortical axis reactivity in acutely depressed psychiatric in-patients, measured by the Dex-CRH test. Kunzel HE, et al. Neuropsychopharmacology. 2003 Dec; 28(12):2169–78.

22. Pole S. Ayurvedic Medicine: The Principles of Traditional Practice. Philadelphia; Elsevier, Churchill Livingstone, 2006: pp133–4.

23. Mills S, Bone K. The Essential Guide to Herbal Safety. St Louis, Missouri; Churchill Livingstone, 2005: pp 578–80

24. Kelly GS. Rhodiola rosea: a possible plant adaptogen. Altern Med Rev. 2001 Jun;6(3): 293–302

25. Pole S. Ayurvedic Medicine: The Principles of Traditional Practice. Philadelphia; Elsevier, Churchill Livingstone, 2006: pp220–1.

26. Banderet LE, Lieberman HR. Treatment with tyrosine, a neurotransmitter precursor, reduces environmental stress in humans. Brain Res Bull. 1989 Apr; 22(4): 759–62.

27. Fisher, H, Arom, A, Brown, L (2005). Romantic Love: An F MRI Study of Neural Mechanism for Mate Choice. Journal of Comparative Neurology. 493 (one), 58–62.

28. Fiona Macrae November 2013.'Cuddle hormone holds the secret to looking beautiful: Whiff of oxytocin makes men find their partners more attractive'. Daily Mail. (http://www.dailymail.co.uk/sciencetech/article-2513594/Cuddle-hormone-Oxytocin-holds-secret-lookingbeautiful.html#ixzz4Am61h0PU).

29. Van Die MD, Burger HG, Teede HJ, Bone KM. Vitex agnus-castus extracts for female reproductive disorders: a systematic review of clinical trials.

Planta Med. 2013 May;79(7): 562–75.

30. Braun L, Cohen, M. Herbs and Natural Supplements. 2nd ed. Chatsworth, News South Wales: Churchill Livingstone, 2007; pp 540–44.

31. Thorpe A, Neal D. Benign prostatic hyperplasia. Lancet. 2003 Apr 19;361(9366): 1359–67

32. Christudoss P, Selvakumar R, Fleming JJ, Gopalakrishnan G. Zinc status of patients with benign prostatic hyperplasia and prostate carcinoma. Indian J Urol. 2011 Jan;27(1):14-8.

33. Hage M et al. The link between Thyroid Function and Depression. Journal of Thyroid Research. 2012; 10:1155; Almeida C et al. Subclinical hypothyroidism: psychiatric disorders and symptoms. 2007; 29(2); 157–9

34. Bauer et al. Thyroid hormones, serotonin and mood: of synergy and significance in the adult brain. Molecular Psychiatry. 2002; 7(2): 140–156

35. Chen HJ, Meites J. Endocrinology. 1975; Vol 96, 10–14.

36. Bauer M et al. The Thyroid-Brain Interaction in Thyroid and Mood Disorders. Journal of Neuroendocrinology. 2008; 20: 1101–1114

37. Rostami R. et al. Effect of zinc deficiency on thyroid hormone synthesis and thyroid antibodies. Clinical Biochemistry. 2011; 44(13): S108

38. Yoon et al. Anti-inflammatory effect of quercetin in a whole orbital tissue culture of Graves' orbitopathy. Br J Ophthalmol. 2012; 96(8):1117–21.

39. Lieberman HR et al. Nutrition, brain function and cognitive performance. Appetite. 2003 40(3)pp. 245–54; Tahara et al. (1985). Nihon Naibunpi Gakkai Zasshi. 61(11) pp. 1270–81.

40. Panda S, Kar A. Changes in thyroid hormone concentrations after administration of ashwagandha root extract to adult male mice. J Pharm Pharmacol. 1998; 50: 1065–1068.

41. Blumenthal M, Senior Editor. The Complete German Commission E Monographs. Therapeutic Guide to Herbal Medicines. Texas; American Botanical Council. 1998: pp160–1.

42. Bone K. The curious case of coleus and the pharmacology of forskolin, parts 1 and 2. MediHerb Professional Review. 1990;numbers 16 (Sept) and 17 (Dec).

43. Psotová J, Kolár M, Sousek J, Svagera Z, Vicar J, Ulrichová J. Biological activities of Prunella vulgaris extract. Phytother Res all all or a web 2003;17(9):1082–7.

44. Managing subclinical hypothyroidism. Australian Prescriber 1999;22(6):132–134.

45. McElduff A, McElduff P, Gunton JE, Hams G, Wiley V, Wilcken BM. Neonatal thyroid-stimulating hormone concentrations in northern Sydney: further indications of mild iodine deficiency? Med J Aust. 2002 Apr 1;176(7):317–20

46. Møller, SE. Serotonin, Carbohydrates and atypical depression, Pharmacol Toxicol. 1992;71 Suppl 1:61–71.
47. Ahima RS, DA Antwi. Brain regulation of appetite and satiety. Endocrinol Metab Clin North Am. 2008 Dec;37(4):811–23.
48. Gregory Morton et al, Leptin and the control of glucose metabolism, Physiology Review. 2012.
49. Sonnenberg Gabriele E, Glenn Matfin, Rickey, Reinhardt. British Journal of Diabetes and Vascular Disease. 2007; 7(3): 111–118
50. Salem, Victoria, Stephen R Bloom. Expert Rev Clin Pharmacol. 2010; 3(1): 73–88.
51. Gerard Karsenty, M.D., Ph.D., chair of the Department of Genetics & Development at Columbia University's College of Physician and Surgeons.
52. Bellesi M. 'Sleep and Oligodendrocyte Functions' Current Sleep Medicine Reports. 2015.
53. Masaro, E, et al. Overview of caloric restriction and ageing. Mech Ageing Dev. 2005 Sep;126(9):913–22.
54. Stewart S et al. Australia's Future 'Fat Bomb'. Baker Heart Research Institute. Melbourne, Australia. 2008.
55. Dulloo AG, et al. Efficacy of a green tea extract rich in catechin polyphenols and caffeine in increasing 24-h energy expenditure and fat oxidation in humans. Am J Clin Nutr. 1999; 70(6):1040–5.
56. Ukkola O et al, Adiponectin: a link between excess adiposity and associated comorbidities, J Mol Med. 2002 Nov;80(11):696–702.
57. Samsel A, Seneff S. Glyphosate's Suppression of Cytochrome P450 Enzymes and Amino Acid Biosynthesis by the Gut Microbiome: Pathways to Modern Diseases. Entropy. 2013. 15(4). 1416–1463
58. Perez Lg, Franz KJ. Minding metals: tailoring multifunctional chelating agents for neurodegenerative disease. Dalton trans. 2010 Mar 7; 39(9): 2177–2187.
59. Dean O, et al. N-acetylcysteine in psychiatry: current therapeutic evidence and potential mechanisms of action. J Psychiatry Neurosci. 2011; 36(2):78–86.
60. Flora SJ, Mittal M, Mehta A. Heavy metal induced oxidative stress and its possible reversal by chelation therapy. Indian J Med Res. 2008 Oct; 128(4)501–523.
61. Delavarian M, Hassanvand A and Gharibzadeh S. Increasing performance in children with ADHD by trapping lead with a nanozeolite. J Neuropsychiatry Clin Neurosci. 2013 Winter; 25(1): E23.
62. Nutrition and Mental Illness: An Orthomolecular Approach to Balancing Body Chemistry Apr 1, 1988 Carl C. Pfeiffer Ph.D. M.D.
63. Basu N, et al. Effects of mercury on neurochemical receptors in wild river otters (Lontra canadensis). Environ Sci Technol. 2005 May 15;39(10): 3585–91.

64. Janakiramaiah N, et al. Antidepressant Efficacy of Sudarshan Kriya Yoga (SKY) in Melancholia, Journal of Affective Disorders (Jan.–March 2000): Vol. 57, No. 1–3, pp. 255–59.

65. Nagarathna R; Nagendra HR. (1985) Yoga for bronchial asthma: a controlled study. Br Med J. (Clin Res Ed). 291(6502): 1077–9.

66. Gelderloos P. et al. (1991) Effectiveness of the Transcendental Meditation program in preventing and treating substance misuse: a review. Jut J. Addict. 26(3): 293–325)

67. Gaston L et al. (1991) Psychological stress and psoriasis: experimental and prospective correlational studies. Acta Derm Venereol Suppl. (Stockholm) 156: 37–43).

68. Alexander CN.et.al. (1989) Transcendental meditation, mindfulness, and longevity: an experimental study with the elderly. J. Pers. Soc Psychol. 57: 950–964.

69. Calabrese F, Rossetti AC, Racagni G, et al. Brain-derived neurotrophic factor: a bridge between inflammation and neuroplasticity. Front Cell Neurosci. 2014; 8: 430.

www.ingramcontent.com/pod-product-compliance
Lightning Source LLC
Chambersburg PA
CBHW071234080526
44587CB00013BA/1609